Five Rivers

The History
of a
Special Place

Five Rivers

The History of a Special Place

Contributing Authors:

RoseAnne Fogarty

Morgan Gmelch

John Smolinsky

Published by

Friends of Five Rivers/Five Rivers Limited

2012

Five Rivers: The History of a Special Place
Copyright © 2012 by Friends of Five Rivers/Five Rivers Ltd.

Cover photo by Martin Turnidge
Book design by Jessika Hazelton

Printed in the United States of America
The Troy Book Makers • Troy, New York • thetroybookmakers.com

To order additional copies of this title,
contact your favorite local bookstore
or visit www.tbmbooks.com

ISBN: 978-1-61468-093-2

Note on the Relationship of
New York State Department of Environmental Conservation's
Five Rivers Environmental Education Center and
Friends of Five Rivers/Five Rivers Ltd.

The relationship between Five Rivers Limited, doing business as the Friends of Five Rivers, and the NYS Department of Environmental Conservation has existed since 1972, when the Five Rivers Environmental Education Center was officially opened. As an independent not-for-profit membership organization, Friends of Five Rivers has the purpose of supporting the educational work of the Center.

The Center provides programs in three areas:
Supplemental education experiences for groups of school-age children;

Interpretive programs for the general public;

Teacher training

Friends of Five Rivers has become an integral part of the center, giving support in several major ways:
Raising funds to support educational programs;

Coordinating a variety of volunteer services;

Handling funds for programs and services such as internships and construction projects;

Providing community contacts;

Giving advice and assistance to the Center staff in a variety of program related matters.

CONTENTS

Preface xi
    By John Smolinsky for Friends of Five Rivers

Foreword xiii
    By Craig Thompson, Director,
    Fiver Rivers Environmental Education Center

Acknowledgments xv
    By RoseAnne Fogarty

Frontispiece xvii
    Five Rivers: A Time Line

Chapter 1: Bedrock 1

Chapter 2: Early Days: Native Americans and Colonists 9

Chapter 3: Trails to Rails to Power Lines 19

Chapter 4: Beginnings of Cinservation:
    Delmar Experimental Game Farm 31

Chapter 5: The Civilian Conservation Corps 41

Chapter 6: The Delmar "Zoo" 53

Chapter 7: The Wildlife Research Center 61

Chapter 8: Conservation Comes of Age:
    Five Rivers Enviornmental Education Center 69

Chapter 9: "The Friends":
    Friends of Five Rivers/Five Rivers Limited 93

Chapter 10: Into the Future 113

Appendix 116

Bibliography 132

Photo by RA Fogarty

PREFACE

BY JOHN SMOLINSKY FOR FRIENDS OF FIVE RIVERS

In a world of electronic devices, crammed schedules, and conflicting priorities it is always a pleasure to find a nearly perfect nexus of peace, nature, friends, and memories. In 2005 an idea emerged to tell a story about such a place, loved by many over the last 75 years. Friends of Five Rivers embarked on a mission to gather the memories of this place, in past times known as the Ackerman Farm, the Game Farm, the CCC Camp, the Delmar Zoo, the Wildlife Research Center, and now Five Rivers Environmental Education Center.

At this place a mix of government, interested citizens, and nature itself has formed an environmental partnership transcending the merely physical past and present. Of this place there are facts to be recorded, stories to be told, and impressions to be shared.

Like the pieces of a puzzle, the facts and stories begin as an impressionistic jumble of memories from many sources. Preparing this book was an exercise in sifting these overlapping tales into a time line of the history of a place, from prehistoric to modern, with emphasis on the developments of the 20th Century and beyond.

The book explains some things you may have wondered about: for example, why was a place with two streams given the name "Five Rivers"? Why is there so much limestone here? Who were the people who used this land over the generations? There is this and more to learn here.

Visitors who come to Five Rivers for environmental education, solitude, or natural outdoor enjoyment can't fail to notice the human marks overlaid on the site. There are rugged wooden buildings, an orchard, some symmetrically dug ponds, walls of large stone blocks. Five Rivers ceased to be wilderness many generations ago. Our appreciation of it as an environment can be enhanced by an understanding of those who preceded us on the land.

Our history of Five Rivers could no doubt be embellished by the thousands of people who have worked at or visited the place over the years. We welcome your knowledge and stories, and will be looking for ways to share them in the future.

Who actually wrote this book? I proposed the original idea in 2006. Morgan Gmelch, a budding anthropologist/historian who visited Five Rivers as a child, teenager, and adult, drafted several chapters. RoseAnne Fogarty, a former president of the board of Friends of Five Rivers, brought the manuscript to completion. Many other members of the Friends and staff of the Center contributed, and are mentioned in the Acknowledgments section.

We hope you enjoy this history of Five Rivers; it's about your special place.

FOREWORD

by Craig D. Thompson, Director,
Five Rivers Environmental Education Center

If Neil Armstrong had found that there were already footprints on the moon when he arrived, would that have intrigued you? Well, I vividly recall finding "footprints" of the past on my first walk around Five Rivers. I have spent the last thirty years trying to understand how they got there. Now, thanks to this history, you can find and begin to appreciate the enriching story they tell.

Strolling Five Rivers' broad fields and brooding forests, the casual visitor frequently encounters anomalies: stone stairways leading nowhere, concrete abutments in a pond, antique farm equipment abandoned in the woods. These anachronisms bear witness to activities that only the landscape remembers.

Today, this 445-acre living museum is widely acclaimed as a compendium of biological, ecological, and scenic diversity. But aside from the Center's diversity and sheer size, there is nothing really special about its natural resources, as engaging as they may be. It's the site's nagging historicism, the profound narrative power of confronting the past, that endows Five Rivers with a vibrant and unique "sense of place," making it more than just another public park or wildlife refuge.

In fact, as you'll soon read, the place we now call Five Rivers has been an important conservation venue for over three-quarters of a century. The work of the Delmar Experimental Game Farm, the Civilian Conservation Corps, and the Wildlife Research Center form a long tradition of excellence in wildlife management. The resonating power of land and place embodied within the site's original architecture, waterworks, and earthworks lend the Center a vital cultural dimension.

These mute touchstones of the past can help us to understand what the site was and how it came to be what it is today, and can ultimately bring to the visitor our principal message: environmental stewardship. Told through the dialogue between the built and natural environments, the Five Rivers story advances the most fundamental values of the New York State Department of Environmental Conservation, and is an integral part of the socio-cultural fabric of the entire Capital community.

The suggestion that this unique historical identity has public value has, at times, been ignored. Now it will at least not be forgotten. Come and look for footprints yourself. I think you'll find it simply fascinating to discover that our past is present at Five Rivers.

Craig Thompson as a young environmental educator at Five Rivers in the early 1980s. (Five Rivers Archives)

ACKNOWLEDGMENTS

BY RoseAnne Fogarty

Like almost everything at Five Rivers, this book has been a cooperative project. At first it seemed like an ambitious and unwieldy undertaking. We could never have brought it to completion without generous contributions of time and expertise from people with special knowledge of the subject.

We would like to especially thank NYS geologist (retired) Robert Fakundiny, for his review of Chapter 1 on the geology of the area, and Bethlehem town historian Susan Leath and New Scotland town historian Robert Parmenter for reading and clarifying Chapters 2 and 3.

Past Five Rivers directors Robert Budliger and Alan Mapes reviewed Chapters 4 through 9, and their firsthand perspective on many events was invaluable. Early Five Rivers Ltd. staffers Grace Weatherby and Geraldine Oakley added much clarity to Chapters 8 and 9. Nancy Payne, a longtime DEC staffer and a dedicated collector of stories enriched the narrative, as did Leda Loux, Friends of Five Rivers administrator for almost twenty years. Elizabeth Manning, editor of *Five Rivers Ramblings* for nine years, also reviewed Chapter 8 and 9. Kitty Rusch of the Center staff, along with Joannne Macklin and Nancy Conway of Friends staff helped bring all the photos and other pieces together.

Photo by Morgan Gmelch

Current Center Director Craig Thompson read the entire manuscript and gave useful input. John Smolinsky, as the originator of the project, also gave the whole book his thoughtful review. Finally, Maggie Moeringer threw herself into the project at the eleventh hour, proofreading the entire manuscript and, along with Friends President Rich Bader, beginning the marketing plan.

For the inevitable errors, the responsibility is mine; I trust the readers to let me know about them. I would also love to hear more tales of our special place, and I know we will find a way to use them.

FIVE RIVERS: A TIME LINE

BP = "before present"; CE = "common era" (formerly AD)

Precambrian Eon	Earth's crust forms.	4 billion BP
Grenville Orogeny	Continental collision creates NYS bedrock, visible in Adirondacks and Hudson Highlands.	950 million BP
Paleozoic Era	NYS is mostly shallow seabed, with invertebrates and later, fish, leaving fossils in sedimentary rock.	540 million BP
Ordovician Period	Shrinking sea leaves Queenston Delta. Arthropods colonize land.	440 million BP
Devonian Period	Tropical conditions encourage propagation of land plants, such as the Gilboa Forest.	370 million BP
Mesozoic Era	Dinosaurs exist in southern NYS counties.	230 million BP to 187 million BP
Cenozoic Era		
Quaternary Period	Ice age glaciers alter NYS landscape as far south as Long Island, covering previous features and lowering sea levels. Humans migrate to North America.	20 thousand BP
	Receding ice sheet leaves Glacial Lake Albany and surrounding tundra, habitat for many mammals.	13 thousand BP
Holocene Epoch	First humans reach Northeastern US.	10 thousand BP
	Maize cultivation is widespread in temperate US.	3 thousand BP
	Permanent settlements are established in Five Rivers area.	3 thousand BP

	Agricultural villages become common.	1 thousand BP
	Bows and arrows and flint tools come into common use around Five Rivers.	6 hundred BP
	Mohicans dominate Five Rivers area. Iroquois-speaking nations form confederacy.	4 hundred BP
	Dutch arrive and establish settlements.	1609 CE
	British take over Dutch colony.	1664 CE
	American Revolution begins.	1775 CE
	Town of Bethlehem is established.	1793 CE
	Town of New Scotland is established.	1832 CE
	Delmar Game Farm is established.	1933 CE
	Five Rivers Environmental Education Center is established.	1972 CE

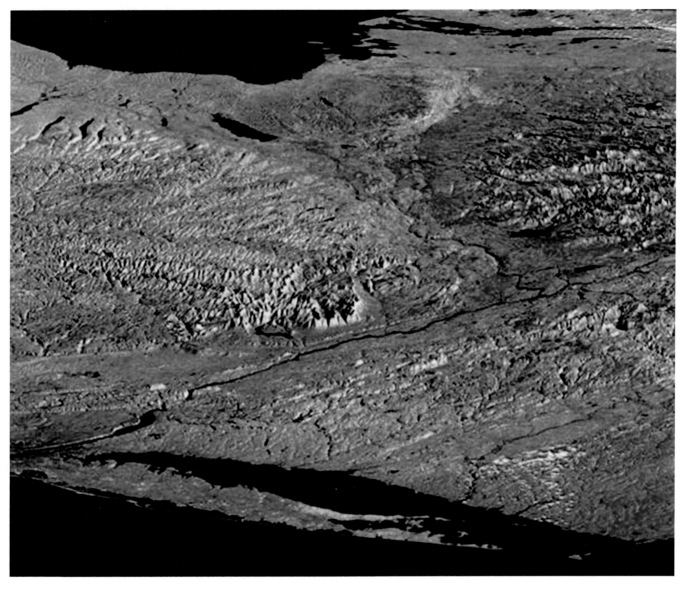

New York State as it appears from a NASA satellite, with the Hudson-Mohawk lowlands in the center right. (National Aeronautic and Space Administration)

CHAPTER 1

BEDROCK

Geology underlies everything:
it founds the landscape, dictates the agriculture,
determines the character of villages.
Geology acts as a kind of
collective unconscious for the world,
a deep control beneath the oceans and continents.
For the general reader,
the most compelling part of geological enlightenment
is discovering what geology does,
how it interacts with natural history,
or the story of our own culture.

Richard Fortey
Earth: An Intimate History

The historical record starts in rock. Imagine Five Rivers first as a tiny spot on the eastern margin of the great mass that would become North America. Made of a granitic gneiss, produced by enormous heat and pressure, much of this proto-North America was covered by shallow seas. This was the shadowy Pre-Cambrian era, stretching from over four billion years ago to a half billion years ago.

With the unimaginable slowness of hundreds of millions of years, continents and ocean floors collided, slid over and under each other, and attached themselves. Land crumpled under impact, formed mountain ranges, and then eroded into lowlands.

During one massive event over a billion years ago, now known as the Grenville Orogeny, another continent and its adjoining oceanic crust slid under the eastern edge of proto-North America, building mountains and plateaus along the collision zone, from Mexico to Canada. These again eroded, but what remained can be seen in New York's bedrock, still visible in the granitic gneiss of the Adirondacks and the Hudson Highlands. The basement rock of our region is this metamorphic rock that is continuous with the rest of North America.

In the course of the following 400 million years of erosion and leveling, other collisions knit all the continents together into one super-continent. These in turn became unstable and split apart. As proto-North America moved away, the rift released volcanic material which gave the continent a new eastern continental shelf. The stage was set for the Paleozoic era, starting more than 500 million years ago.

This brachiopod fossil reflects one of the many life forms common to the shallow sea covering the Five Rivers area five to six hundred million years ago. (Photo by RA Fogarty)

The New York State Museum's Educational Leaflet # 68, *Geology of New York: A Simplified Account,* provides a fascinating overview of this period. Describing the mid-Paleozoic Era, it notes:

> *New York State itself was a quiet sea basin, much like the shallow ocean between Australia and New Guinea today.... Invertebrate organisms dominated the seas in the Cambrian, Ordovician, and Silurian Periods. Fish— the first vertebrates—had appeared in the late Cambrian. By the end of the Silurian, they had become relatively abundant. (p. 98)*

All along the eastern lowlands and the new shelf, then, warm shallow waters became filled with early aquatic life forms. Thick sediments accumulated, filled with the remains of these creatures. Fossils of trilobites, sea lilies, corals, and early mollusks and fish can still be found in deeply cut streambeds in the Bethlehem/New Scotland area, delighting the observant hiker.

Life on Land

Eventually, with erosion of the highlands, what had been coastal shallows became a delta, forerunner of the "Five Rivers" valley that was to come. *Geology of New York* describes the rich diversity and abundance of life in the shallow and shrinking sea that was being filled by the Late Ordovician delta that would be known as the Queenston Delta.

> *With such intense competition, it is hardly surprising that life began to move into a different environment at this time. Air-breathing arthropods (insects, spiders, etc.) began to evolve. They eventually colonized the land in the Late Silurian. (pp.98-99)*

So along the edges of the emerging land, rare land plants and then primitive animals similar to millipedes and spiders began to appear. Then the first air-breathing, four-legged amphibians ventured onto land. Try to imagine this development of sentient land animals occurring over a period of 200 million years.

One of the oldest fossil forests on earth, Gilboa Forest was uncovered in the 1920s when Blenham-Gilboa Dam on the Schoharie Creek was constructed. In this photo, the remaining trunk footprints from the forest's trees look like small volcanoes in the sedimentary rock. The strings crisscrossing the site give scale: each quadrant is 1.5 meters by 2.5 meters. The forest flourished about 350 million years ago, on the shore of the coastal sea that covered the Five Rivers area. (Courtesy of Dr. William E. Stein)

Moving into the Devonian period of 350 million years ago, the climate was humid and hot, perfect for forests of fernlike trees. Visitors to the area can actually see fossils of such trees near Gilboa, along the Schoharie Creek: the so-called Gilboa forest, first exposed when the Blenham-Gilboa Reservoir was excavated.

Did dinosaurs stalk through this tropical forest? We don't know; New York's fossil record for land organisms is limited. Fossil dinosaur tracks and teeth from the Mesozoic Era have been found to the south in Rockland County. Sites to the south and east in Connecticut, Massachusetts, Long Island, Staten Island, and New Jersey have also yielded evidence of early plants and vertebrates, including birds and marine crocodile-like animals. But not the Hudson-Mohawk Lowlands. The reason may lie in a major shift that wiped away previous evidence while leaving its own marks on upstate New York, marks that persist to the present.

The rock exposed along the deeply cut Vlomankill is sedimentary, (greywacke, sandstone, siltstone, and shale) and shows the effects of later pressure and up-heaval in its slanted orientation. This shows that it is from the earlier Ordovician deposits left by the coastal sea, rather than from the later Glacial Lake Albany. (Photo by RA Fogarty)

The Ice Sheet

The primary feature of central and northern New York's geology today is the impact of the Laurentide Ice Sheet, which advanced south to cover the area. At its maximum reach about 22,000 years ago, it spread as far as northern Long Island. In our area the ice sheet was perhaps two kilometers thick, easily sliding over the top of the Helderbergs. Over the next 12,000 years, the ice sheet slowly receded and advanced in ever-smaller waves. The glacial processes eroded, moved, and reformed the surfaces left behind, leaving deep layers of glacial till and melt-water.

One such vast collection of water overspread today's Capital Region and is referred to as Glacial Lake Albany. It was 320 kilometers long, stretching from Glens Falls to New York City, and was 120 meters deep at Albany. When the lake eventually drained to the south, it left broad deltas of sand and debris. One such delta covers the Hudson Mohawk Lowland area of which Five Rivers is a part. The Albany-Schenectady Pine Bush is a prime example of a concentrated sand deposit from that time. Its sand delta was formed mostly by sediment brought down the Mohawk during the massive flood of water released from glacial Lake Iroquois, as the receding ice sheet removed the ice dam that held it back.

The shores of the receding Lake Albany 13,000 years ago would have been cold, dry tundra, gradually giving way over the next two millennia to spruce and fir forest. This habitat became home to a plethora of warm blooded species: mammoths and mastodons, ground sloths, peccary, bison, giant beaver, Cali-

Discovered in 1866 near Cohoes Falls on the Mohawk River, the Cohoes Mastodon was a young male weighing between 8,000 and 10,000 pounds. The NYS Museum Website states that "it had been in poor health and may have died a natural death, although some research on the skeleton hints that it may have been killed by Native American hunters." (Copyright New York State Museum)

fornia condors, and still others, some of which remain today. Scientists theorize that the extinction of many of these Pleistocene Epoch animals may have been hastened by the arrival in the area of humans.

First Humans

Current thinking is that the oceans were perhaps 300 feet lower during the Ice Age, permitting humans to cross a land bridge at "Beringia" a now-submerged stretch of land between Siberia and Alaska. The earliest human remains found on this continent, in the northwest, have been dated to about 14,000 years ago. Dates in this field of study are often debated, of course, and are subject to ongoing revision.

The migrations of humans spread south and east, reaching what is now the Northeastern United States around 12,500 years ago, or perhaps even earlier. By this time, the culture of early peoples was differentiated by climatic regions, with fishing along the coasts and rivers, and hunting and gathering in forests.

By 3,000 years ago maize cultivation had spread to what would be the temperate areas of the United States, and by about 1,400 years ago, bow and arrow use was making hunting more efficient, and flint hoes were replacing digging sticks. We turn to the story of the first human settlers to the Five Rivers area in Chapter 2.

The Archaic people who hunted in New York and southern Ontario during the late Ice Age are referred to as the Laurentian Archaic. Thought to have no settled villages, they lived by hunting, fishing, and gathering, using a variety of chipped and polished stone tools. (Copyright New York State Museum)

Chapter 1 Resources

Faragher, John Mack, et al. *Out of Many: A History of the American People (5th Edition)*. Pearson/Prentice Hall: Upper Saddle River, NJ, 2009

Fortey, Richard. *Earth: An Intimate History*. NY: Alfred A. Knopf, 2004

Isachsen, Y.W. et al. (Eds.) *Geology of New York: A Simplified Account (2nd Edition)*. Albany, NY: New York State Museum: Education Leaflet # 28, 2000

Landing, Ed. *Fossils and "Deep Time" in New York*. Albany, NY: New York State Museum, 2004.

New York State Dept of Environmental Conservation. *Five Rivers Environmental Education Center: Draft Unit Management Plan*. Albany County: Towns of New Scotland and Bethlehem, February 2007.

Thompson, Ida. *National Audubon Society Field Guide to North American Fossils*. NY: Alfred A. Knopf, 1995

Titus, Robert. *The Catskills in the Ice Age*. Fleischmanns, NY: Purple Mountain Press, 1990

Van Diver, Bradford B. *Field Guide: Upstate New York*. (K/H Geology Field Guide Series) Toronto: Kendall/Hunt Publishing Company, 1980

Van Diver, Bradford B. *Roadside Geology of New York*. Missoula, MT: Mountain Press Publishing Company, 1985.

Weishampel, David B. and Young, Luther. *Dinosaurs of the East Coast*. Baltimore: Johns Hopkins University Press, 1996.

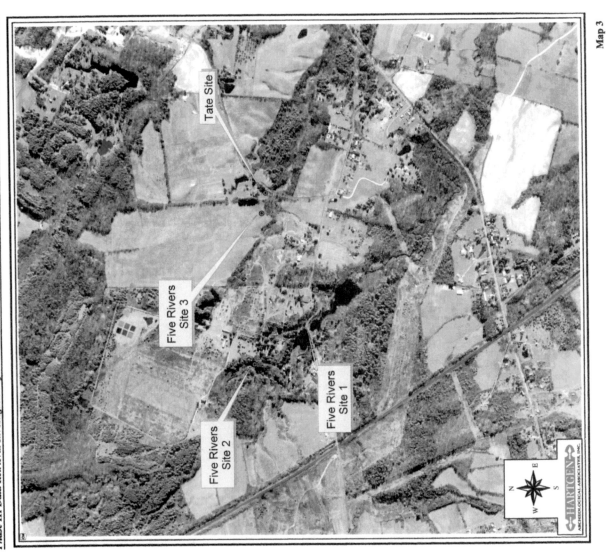

Map 3

Maps of Five Rivers Sites and Tate Site

1999 NYSDOS *New York State 2000 Digitally Enhanced Ortho Imagery*

March 2002

Hartgen Archeological Associates, Inc.

A proposal to install water and sewer lines precipitated a 2002 study of Five Rivers and the nearby Tate house focused on finding evidence of Native American or earlier occupancy of the area. According to the final report, "The tight grouping of sites found with Five Rivers including the Tate Site supports the interpretation that the Five Rivers region was a focal point for pre-contact occupation." (Courtesy of Hartgen Archeological Associates)

CHAPTER 2

EARLY DAYS:

NATIVE AMERICANS AND COLONISTS

We sometimes in traveling...
find ourselves on high elevated situations,
from which we overlook large portions of country....
Here our attention is arrested
in the beautiful landscape around us....
...on the hills, at the brooks, and in the valleys,
where the game abounds and where the deer are feeding,
or gamboling or resting in the shadows in full view

Adriaen Van Der Donck
A Description of New Netherlands
1653

The earliest people to live in America, known only from archaeological evidence, are referred to as Paleo-Indians. As the glaciers retreated, these nomadic hunters and foragers followed major river valleys into the Northeast from south and west, leaving behind occasional tools at their temporary camps and kill sites. During the Early, Middle, and Late Archaic Periods (10,000 to 4,000 years ago) people made regular seasonal forays into our area from base camps in milder climates to the south. Over time there was a gradual loss of large North American animal species, and scientists now hypothesize that over-hunting as well as climate change may have contributed to the demise of these species.

Evidence of the Archaic people, including the distinctive Clovis points (associated with the Paleo-Indian Clovis culture of 13,000 BPE), has been found in aboriginal sites in the Town of Bethlehem, but permanent settlements were not established until about 3,500 years ago. The land was then covered with mixed hardwood forests, interspersed with some spruce, hemlock, and pine. Deer, bear, moose, beaver, mink, raccoon, woodchuck, turkey, and passenger pigeon abounded, and were hunted and trapped . Acorns, nuts, plants, and berries filled out the Native Americans' diet. Fish were plentiful in rivers and streams, especially during the spring herring and shad runs up the Hudson.

The Mohican people occupying the region before the arrival of the Dutch used maize, beans, and squash as complementary plantings. They burned off forest and scrub to open up new areas for planting, a practice that made sense when land was abundant. (Copyright New York State Museum)

The shift from an exclusively hunter/gatherer culture to agricultural villages had taken place by the year 1000 CE, and a number of village sites have been found along the Hudson and Mohawk Rivers. These villages of about 200 people grew maize, beans, and squash, drying and storing any surplus for winter use. Like many peoples worldwide with "land to burn," they practiced slash and burn agriculture. Fires were set to clear space for planting; the practice also destroyed forest undergrowth, opening up the countryside for hunting and travel.

In late fall, family groups left their villages to travel up creeks like the Normanskill and the Vlomankill to hunt, leaving the elders behind. After returning to the villages for mid-winter, the men would go out again in March to hunt moose. Every eight to twelve years, as garden plots became less fertile, wood became scarce, and debris accumulated, the villagers would move to a new location.

At the time of the Dutch arrival, the Mohicans dominated our immediate area. Historian Shirley Dunn notes that by 1609 the Algonquian-speaking Mohicans controlled the land from what is now Dutchess and Ulster Counties north to Saratoga and Washington Counties, and from western Massachusetts to the Catskills

The New York State Museum's model Iroquois village provides a sense of how the Mohawk and Mohican villages would have looked, with longhouses on a hilltop surrounded by a stockade. (Copyright New York State Museum)

and the Helderbergs. The Iroquoian-speaking Mohawks then occupied a broad expanse of the Mohawk Valley, sometimes hunting north into the Adirondacks and south to the Oneonta area.

Both groups were somewhat sedentary, occupying hilltop villages near rivers, with substantial longhouses of hickory saplings covered with bark. They began to surround their villages with defensive stockades as competition for resources and trade routes increased. More than 100 years before European contact, the Iroquois Confederacy was formed by the Mohawks, the Oneidas, the Onondagas, the Cayugas, and the Senecas in response to inter-tribal conflict and territorial expansion.

Five Rivers is relatively flat and low (generally less that 240 feet above sea level), cut by the Vlomankill and Phillipinkill creeks. Though there is no evidence of a permanent Native American settlement, it was clearly used for hunting and gathering.

According to George Baker, who grew up on the "Delmar Game Farm" (see Chapter 4), the current North Loop Trail encompasses what "used to be a wheat field. My father used to take me out there and we would walk through the freshly plowed field and pick up all kinds of arrowheads, spear points, hatchet heads, things like that. My father developed quite a collection just from that one field."

Within a two mile radius of Five Rivers archaeologists have found seventeen pre-contact sites. One of these, to the east of the Phillipinkill, contained chert flakes, cores, and other tool debris. Another pre-contact site was found within a mile of Five Rivers, and a third on Five Rivers property. So far, however, it appears that Five Rivers was used by Native Americans only seasonally.

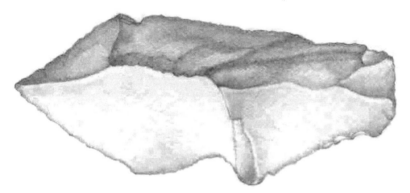

This "unifacial knife" was unearthed at Site 1 on the Hartgen map featured at the beginning of this chapter, near what is now the beginning of the Woodlot Trail. (Courtesy of Hartgen Archeological Associates)

European Settlement

In September 1609, Henry Hudson, explorer and employee of the Dutch East India Company, sailed up the Hudson to a point near the Mohican village of Schotak. There he met a Mohican chief "who carried him to his house and made him good cheere." Hudson traded beads, knives, and hatchets for beaver and otter skins, and was given strings of shell beads—a sign of respect.

At this time, according to anthropologist T.J. Brasser, there were three Mohican towns in the area: one near the confluence of the Mohawk and Hudson Rivers, one near what would become Fort Orange, and the one in "Schotak."

Several Dutch trading expeditions followed. The Dutch signed treaties with both the Mohicans and the Mohawks, and established a trading post on Castle Island in the Hudson, the first European structure in what would become the Town of Bethlehem. Later, in 1624, Fort Orange was built at the current site of Albany.

The Albany area quickly became a center of Native American-European trade in furs, especially beaver, and this led inevitably to competition between the Mohicans and the Mohawks. Both wanted the steel tools and weapons the Dutch provided, but Mohawks had to cross Mohican territory to trade. Initial conflicts resulted in an agreement whereby the Mohawks would pay a toll to cross Mohican territory. Ultimately, though, the Mohicans were pushed east, establishing themselves on the east side of the Hudson, and the Mohawks came to dominate the west bank of the Hudson, including the Five Rivers area.

This recent painting by Len Tantillo, "Fort Orange and the Patroons House," captures the early Dutch settlement's focus on trade, with its tightly clustered headquarters buildings and ships arriving and departing. (Courtesy of Len Tantillo)

Adriaen Van Der Donck: An Early Naturalist

The first book written about what would become New York State is a remarkable little natural history and anthropology of the Five Rivers region. Adriaen Van Der Donck was a young man who came to Rensselaerwyck as a "schout," defined by his translator as "a resident officer charged with guarding the Patroon's legal rights and administering justice in the colony." Van Der Donck must have kept a detailed journal, and each chapter of his book covers one aspect of the "enchanting prospects" he encountered every day.

His chapters include one on the local people, describing the custom of "bush burning" for agriculture. Other chapters detail the native trees and plants, the wild animals, the fish and "poisons" (snakes and lizards), and the local soil and minerals. An entire chapter is devoted to the beaver. Van Der Donck wrote eloquently about the birds, especially "whiteheads" (bald eagles), "birds of a lustrous blue color," and "a bird about the length of a finger" that "sucks its nourishment from flowers," and "makes a humming noise."

The book was published in the Nether-

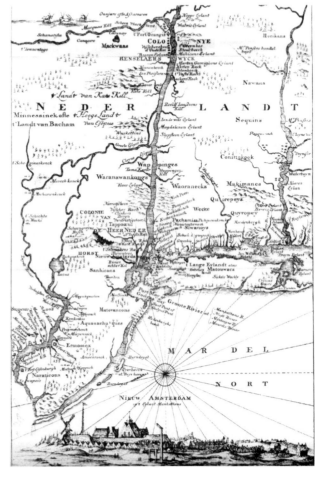

An early map of New Netherlands published in 1656 by Evert Nieuwenhof, Bookseller in the second edition of Adriaen Van Der Donck's book. (Map from the 1968 reprint of Van Der Donck, edited by Thomas F. O'Donnell, and published by Syracuse University Press.)

lands in 1653, two years before the author's premature death. By that time, he was known as an activist who had tried to expose and correct the Dutch mismanagement of the colony that would ultimately result in a British takeover.

In 1841, Jeremiah Johnson did the valuable service of translating Van Der Donck's book into English, giving current American readers the chance to share his fresh and fascinating views of this area.

Patroons and Tenants

During the Mohican/Mohawk struggle for trade dominance, the Dutch had introducing the patroonship system for colonization, granting land within 16 miles of any navigable stream to a patroon (landlord/patron) who would establish a colony of 50 people within four years. In 1630 Killian Van Rensselaer received a charter for lands on both sides of the Hudson around Fort Orange, including some sold to him by the Mohicans. He then, through his agents on the spot, began renting out farms to tenants. According to historian David Ellis

> "The 'durable lease,' the most commonly used, was in perpetuity. Farmers on Van Rensselaer manor had to pay the patroon a perpetual rent of between ten and fourteen bushels of winter wheat per one hundred acres, four fat fowl, and a days work with a team of horses or oxen." (p. 159)

The patroonship system proved remarkably durable. In 1664 the British took over New Netherlands as part of a treaty ending decades of British-Dutch hostilities over land and trade. But the British acknowledged Rensselaerwijck as privately owned and granted it the legal status of an English manor, giving it considerable autonomy. Thus this area retained its predominantly Dutch character as late as the American Revolution.

The first mill on the Vlomankill, near its outlet to the Hudson, had been built in 1640 by Andries de Vos. The first local surnames that appear include Jacob, Bradt (or Bratt), La Grange, Winne, Van Wie, and Slingerland. An early map of the Five Rivers vicinity shows the home of an Adrian Bradt on the Vlomankill, possibly on the foundation of the current Five Rivers "farmhouse," now used as a residence for environmental interns.

The Native American tragedy to be repeated across North America—displacement, disease, and disenfranchisement—was foreshadowed early in New York. By the 1870s Native Americans were feeling severe pressure as permanent settlements began to replace trading posts. In 1675 a peace treaty between the British and the Mohicans and Mohawks should have improved the Native Americans' situation. However, the ravages of smallpox and other diseases introduced from Europe reduced their numbers. They complained that they were forced to sell more land than they intended, to rent from "the Christians," and to pay in produce they could not spare.

By 1700 the Hudson Valley was already home to 100,000 Europeans and fewer than 3000 Native Americans.

The Ackerman Farmhouse stands on a stone foundation supporting large roughhewn beams. Those beams, and the hand-dug well (recently filled in), attest to the age of the structure, which probably predated the Civil War. Early maps show another house existing on or near this site in 1767, belonging to Dutch immigrant Adrain Bradt.
(Photo above by Morgan Gmelch, photo right by RA Fogarty)

Chapter 2 Resources

Baker, George. Interviewed by Dan Ruge. Albany, NY: Five Rivers Archives, June 23, 1993.

Basser, T.J. "Mahican." In *The Handbook of North American Indians.* 15:198-212. Washington, DC: Government Printing Office, 1978.

Bicentennial History Committee, Floyd I. Brewer, Senior Editor. *Bethlehem Revisited: A Bicentennial History, 1793-1993.* Bethlehem Bicentennial Commission, 1993.

Burke, Thomas E. *Mohawk Frontier: The Dutch Community of Schenectady, NY 1661-1710.* Ithaca, NY: Cornell University Press, 1991.

Collamer and Associates, Inc. *Stage 1A and Stage 1B Cultural Resource Investigations for Five Rivers Environmental Education Center, Wildlife Resources Center, Delmar Waterline Project.* (114 Gardner Hill, East Nassau, NY 12062) September 30, 1992

Dunn, Shirley. *The Mohican World, 1680-1750.* Fleischmanns, NY: Purple Mountain Press, 2000.

Dunn, Shirley. *The Mohicans and Their Land, 1609-1730.* Fleischmanns, NY: Purple Mountain Press, 1994.

Eisenstadt, Peter (Ed.) *The Encyclopedia of New York State.* Syracuse, NY Syracuse University Press, 2005

Ellis, David M. et al. *A History of New York State.* Ithaca, NY: NYS Historical Association with Cornell University Press, 1957

Hartgen Archaeological Associates, Inc. *Archaeological Field Reconnaisance for NYDEC.* (1744 Washington Ave. Extension, Rensselaer, NY 12144) March 1999.

Hartgen Archaeological Associates, Inc. *The Tate Site: Phase III Data Retrieval Investigation.* (1744 Washington Ave. Extension, Rensselaer, NY 12144) March 2002.

Jennings, Francis. "Dutch and Swedish Indian Policies." In *The Handbook of North American Indians.* 4:13-19. Washington, DC: Government Printing Office, 1988

Kim, Sung Bok. *Landlord and Tenant in Colonial New York: Manorial Society, 1664-1775.* Chapel Hill, NC: University of North Carolina Press, 1978

NYS Department of Environmental Conservation. *Five Rivers Environmental Education Center: Draft Unit Management Plan: Albany County, Towns of New Scotland and Bethlehem.* February 2007.

Ruttenber, E.M. *Indian Tribes of Hudson's River to 1700.* Saugerties, NY: Hope Farm Press (2nd edition reprint, original 1872), 1998

Van Der Donck, Adriaen. *A Description of the New Nethelands.* Syracuse, NY: Syracuse University Press (published in Dutch in 1653, translated to English by Jeremiah Johnson c. 1841), 1968.

The "Jones Barn" was part of the first property purchased from the Ackermans by the state for the Game Farm. In summer it is home to hundreds of brown bats, a species currently under study for white nose syndrome. (Photo by RA Fogarty)

CHAPTER 3

TRAILS TO RAILS TO POWER LINES

You must teach your children that the ground beneath their feet
is the ashes of your grandfathers.
So that they will respect the land, tell your children
that the earth is rich with the lives of our kin.
Teach your children what we have taught our children,
that the earth is our mother.
Whatever befalls the earth befalls the sons of the earth.
If men spit upon the ground, they spit upon themselves.

Native American Wisdom

The Five Rivers area in the 18th Century reflected the larger region in its shift from Native Americans to Europeans, from Dutch to increasing numbers of English and others, from fur trade to agriculture. The deer paths and Indian trails were giving way to muddy traces cut by horses and riders, and later by wagons.

The process was initially slow. As late as the mid-19th century, less than one acre in ten in the township was "improved" for farming or other use, most roads were unpaved, and railroads

Men from the area fought in the revolution and are buried near the Center. This historic marker is on Fisher Boulevard, less than half a mile from the Center, and the Olivers and the Sagers, along with the Radleys and the Joneses, were among the first actual settlers on the land that now comprises Five Rivers. (Photo by RA Fogarty)

were still in the future. Yet by the end of the century, the land that would become Five Rivers Environmental Education Center was hemmed in, in all directions, by improved roads and railroads. Electrification would soon follow.

Farming

The shift to English control in the 1660s did not eliminate the Rensselaerwyck patroonship, though the name changed to Rensselaer Manor. The ethnic mix began to shift, however. By 1767, according to *Bethlehem Revisited: A Bicentennial History,* the census of Bethlehem's taxpayers shows 200 Dutch, 40 British, 39 German, 18 French Huguenot, and 21 "uncertain." To the Bradts, Louaks, Sagers, and Van Deusens settled in the Five Rivers area were added names like Oliver and Bullock, Radley and Jones.

Development tended to follow the water courses, and spread out from creeks like the Normanskill and the Vlomankill. *Bethlehem Revisited* describes the area before the Revolution as

...heavily agricultural, with a few sawmills, gristmills, and fulling [felting] mills on the principal creeks and an occasional blacksmith, wheelwright, storekeeper, dockowner, or other tradesman or merchant necessary to the farming communities. (p. 58)

Following the commercial tradition of the Dutch, most farmers were interested in raising cash crops. New York wheat fed the Continental Army. Other cash crops were rye, barley, oats, hemp, flax, corn, potatoes, apples, and peas.

During the Revolution the area supplied men as well as crops. Near Fisher Blvd., a short distance east of Five Rivers, are the graves of two Revolutionary soldiers, John Oliver and John Sager, whose family names appear at Five Rivers on early maps.

The Hudson Valley changed hands in the course of the Revolution, and no doubt the British army as well as Washington's soldiers ate the wheat, peas, and apples supplied by the farms of the area.

With its mix of ethnicities, its Tory sympathizers and Revolutionaries, its Native Americans, African enslaved and manumitted people, and bound servants, the area was fairly diverse for what might seem an agricultural backwater. The town of Bethlehem was established in 1793. By the turn of the century, Bethlehem had a population of 3,823. Ten years later, it had risen to 4,430. By 1830,

Curiously, this 1776 map of the "Mannor of Rensselaer" shows the first major creek that enters the Hudson south of the Normanskill (probably the Vlomankill) with the name "Bethlehem Kill." This suggests that the British occupancy of the area included an effort to Anglicize some of the place names. (Map of the Province of New York by C.J. Sauthier and B. Ratzer, engraved by William Faden, 1776). (Reproduced with permission of the New Scotland Historical Association)

the census showed 6,082. It is important to note that Bethlehem included what is now New Scotland until 1832, when a separate township of New Scotland was established.

Slavery in New York

Slavery had been well established for 100 years in upstate New York by the time of the Revolution, and may have been waning. Large landowners and wealthy townsmen held enslaved people as members of their households, but the smaller tenant farmers probably lacked either the capital or the need for much of such labor. The limited land available to a given tenant and the short growing season didn't lend themselves to plantation agriculture. Black tenant farmers were among those farming in Bethlehem, some enslaved and some perhaps manumitted.

The Bethlehem town census of 1800 lists 254 slaves and 13 "free colored." New York law abolished slavery gradually in the first quarter of the 19th Century. Records do exist, however, of the births of children in slavery in 1800, and the auctioning of slaves in the area as late as 1814. The 1820

The Census of the Town of Bethlehem reveals that as late as 1820, slavery was still not uncommon in Bethlehem households. Some families also housed "free colored" people, probably as servants and farm workers. The coding following the appellation indicated gender and age group. So for example the household of Jane Becker included ten free colored people: two elderly males, four female children, a female adult, and three elderly females. The household of Timothy Bussing included two teenage/young adult slaves: one male and one female. (From Records of the Town of Bethlehem, courtesy of the Bethlehem Public Library)

census still showed a few households with as many as five to eight slaves.

Even after New York's abolition of slavery, people escaping slavery in other states were not safe in the United States due to the Fugitive Slave Law. They had to be secretly shuttled to Canada, many of them through this area.

The Underground Railroad History Project of the Capital Region sponsors seminars and tours and encourages ongoing research. Their website can connect the reader to a growing body of knowledge on this aspect of upstate New York's history.

The Five Rivers area remained largely agricultural through the 19th Century. The soil was considered excellent for farming: wheat, dairy, vegetables, and fruit were major products, and many farms also grew fodder and hops. Around 1850, succumbing to the pressures of the long-running Anti-Rent War, the Van Rensselaers began to divest themselves of much of their property in the West Manor through real estate investor Walter

The Tate house on Orchard St. near Five Rivers is a well preserved example of an early home in the Five Rivers vicinity. The "eyebrow" windows on the second floor are a tipoff to the house's antiquity. Until recently it was the home of James Tate, once president of the Board of Five Rivers Ltd. and also known for his pumpkin sale every fall. (Photo by RA Fogarty)

Church, who sold most farms to their tenants during this period. Thus, over the next few decades, ended what author Henry Christman called "despotic medieval landlordism" (p. 305) in the area of the old patroonship.

The table below shows the major trends in agricultural land use in the county in the second half of the 19th Century.

YEAR	FARMS IN ALBANY CO.	ACREAGE IN FARMING
1850	2,903	297,382
1900	3,281 (13 % increase)	298,650 (0.4 % increase)

Note that though the number of farms increased by over ten percent by 1900, acreage in cultivation increased only negligibly. The family farms were being split up among children, but not expanding significantly. Smaller farms were less viable as a way of living, and other businesses and industries were displacing farming. The Five Rivers land itself would come from several bought-out farms.

Lumbering

Until legislation abolished the tenant-landlord system in 1846, the majority of residents in the

"West Manor" were still tenants of the Van Rensselaers. The scale of agriculture was small, constrained by the need to clear every acre. The abundance of wooded land was both a boon and a bane to the settlers. Claiming agricultural land for grazing, grain, and orchards meant clearing forest. Transport of farm produce meant cutting roads through brush and trees.

On the other hand, wood was the primary fuel for cooking, heating, and early industries like charcoal and potash making. It was a primary building material. One history notes that "Practically every farmer was also a lumberman." Churches and schools were built of wood. Farmers built their homes, barns, and fences and fashioned their tools out of wood.

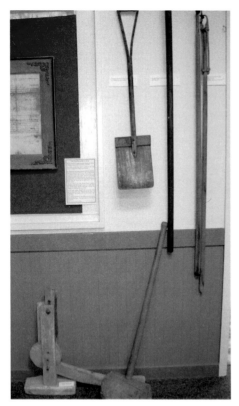

Left: In the absence of metals, and blacksmiths to work them, early farmers took advantage of the abundance of wood for their tools. These tools: a barn shovel, a barley fork, a flail, a wagon wheel jack, and a mallet, are made entirely of wood. (Courtesy of the New Scotland Historical Association)

Above: Even after iron wheels and other parts became available, wood continued to be used for many components, because of economy and ease of manufacture, as with this wooden wine press and seed drill. (Courtesy of the New Scotland Historical Association)

Tapping sugar maples for sap spawned an early industry with varied and interesting paraphernalia. Shown here is some of the sugaring equipment collected by Mary Lou Riccardo, an instructor at Five Rivers who helped to initiate the "Maples" program held every March at Five Rivers. (Photo by RA Fogarty)

Burned-over clearings yielded ash to make lye and potash for fertilizer and soap. Bark was harvested for tanning. Maples were tapped for syrup.

Wood and lumber were also cash merchandise, of course, for those who could get them to market. Wood became the fuel for the steam-boats on the Hudson (starting with Fulton's in 1807), and the railroads that would flank the Five Rivers area. Because trees were such a universally valued commodity for 250 years, New York has few old-growth forests anywhere in the state. None at all exist in the Five Rivers area.

Road Building

For the earliest inhabitants, both Native Americans and Europeans, water courses were the easiest pathways to follow. But they had limitations. Nathaniel Parker Willis, writer and magazine editor in the mid-1800s, reported in 1851 that ice closed the Hudson to navigation well south of Albany for between 70 and 112 days in each of the previous ten years. Clearly, development of the interior and its resources would depend on the painful process of clearing overland roads, and then gradually improving their quality.

The first real roads in the area were created in the late 1700s and early 1800s. Many developed from aboriginal trails and the paths that existed between settlers farms. These were widened to allow the use of horse-drawn wagons, and then the most traveled routes were developed into turnpikes and "paved" with planks, and later stones and gravel. These were maintained by new turnpike companies and paid for by user tolls.

In 1805, the Albany-Delaware Turnpike Company was chartered, establishing the road that became Delaware Avenue. The Albany-Rensselaerville-Schoharie Plank Road Company, chartered in

Right: New Scotland Town Hall, formerly a school building, stands on the site of a still older log school that was the first in the Five Rivers area. There was also a wood frame school at Unionville, near the site of the current Unionville Fire Station. Until compulsory attendance laws were introduced late in 1874, a farm child's education might consist of only a few months a year for a few years. (Photo by RA Fogarty)

Below: The New Scotland Presbyterian Church was built in 1791 on this site, and then rebuilt in 1849. It and the Union Church (built in 1825 and later called the Unionville Reformed Church) were the closest to the Five Rivers site, and they perhaps shared its families among the two congregations. Radleys, Sagers, Bradts, Ackermans, and Joneses are buried in the cemetery of the New Scotland church. (Photo by RA Fogarty)

1859, laid out sections of what is now New Scotland Avenue.

The map below, drawn by cartographer and later railroad magnate Jay Gould in 1854, shows the early development of roads flanking the Five Rivers area.

Railroads

In the 1850s, railroad companies began leasing rights-of-way for building railroads in Bethlehem and New Scotland. The Albany and Susquehanna Railroad opened in 1863, passing through Bethlehem and out through New Scotland. Through a merger this would later become the Delaware and Hudson. In 1865 the Athens and Saratoga (now New York Central) Railroad was constructed, flanking the Five Rivers area on the southwest.

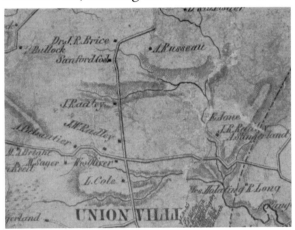

These rail lines, along with the turnpikes now known as Delaware and New Scotland Avenues, effectively set tight boundaries around the open space that we now know as Five Rivers and its adjoining neighbors. They also set the stage for continued development of Albany County and points west.

This detail from an 1854 map by railroad entrepreneur Jay Gould and I. Moore shows the names of the landowners in the Five Rivers area in the mid-19th Century. (Courtesy of the New Scotland Historical Association)

Electrification

Electric power as well as telephone service came to the townships of Bethlehem and New Scotland late in the 1800s, at first only to thickly settled areas. Delmar resident Merle Oliver remembers the homestead of his maternal grandparents, John and Mary Martt, who sold 15 acres to the NYS Conservation Department between 1934 and 1937. That land would become part of Five Rivers on the south side of Game Farm Road. Oliver recalls visiting the farm during the 1920's, when he was a child.

They still drew their water from a well with a well sweep, and they had no electricity. I remember the oil lamps. They had chickens and a cow. I remember my grandmother churning to make butter. They grew everything. My grandfather still had an old muzzle-loader, and I remember him posing for a photograph with it.

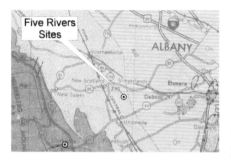

This map illustrates the challenge of dwindling open space in the Five Rivers area. By the turn of the 19th Century all the roads and railroads surrounding Five Rivers were already in place. By the turn of the 20th Century, there was virtually no more affordable open land around Five Rivers to add to the Center. (Courtesy of Hartgen Archeological Associates)

In *More Times Remembered* local historian Allison Bennett mentions a farm in Feura Bush that was electrified in 1926, so power lines were apparently being extended during the 1920s. By the time the Experimental Game Farm was established at the Five Rivers site in 1933, electricity had arrived on site, because photographs of the Civilian Conservation Corps barracks show electric lights (although the power may have been generated on-site).

Turning Points

In the northeastern United States, the 19th Century saw a long but accelerating shift from open space, farming, and lumbering, to industry around urban and suburban areas. It was the industrial Northeast, with its mills and railroads, that became one of the poles of the Civil War debate.

The Civil War affected many families associated with Five Rivers. Town records list Adam, Francis, Henry, John, and William Bradt as serving in the Union Army, as well as Aaron J., Andrew, and George W. Oliver, Conrad Sager, and Christian Ackerman. The area also saw a major influx of German and Irish immigrants during the 1850s and 60s, suggesting what a time of adjustment this must have been for this still rural area.

Before mid-century, industry in Bethlehem and New Scotland consisted mostly of sawmills, gristmills, tanning and blacksmithing. In the second half of the 19th Century, the townships saw the opening of an ice company, an iron works, a printing plant, and a gravel quarry, as well as a commercial dairy, a cider works, a coal distribution company, and numerous hotels and stores.

Advances in industrialization, transportation, and communications were driving accelerating change. By the last decades of the 1800s, some New Yorkers were beginning to think of open land not merely as something to exploit, but also as a resource to preserve.

Chapter 3 Resources

Adams, Arthur G. *The Hudson Throught the Years (2ⁿᵈ Edition)*. New York: Fordham University Press, 1996.

Bennett, Allison. *Times Remembered*. Salem, MS: Higginson Book Company, 1984.

Bennett, Allison. *More Times Remembered*. Salem, MS: Higginson Book Company, 1987.

Berlin, Ira and Harris, Leslie M. (Eds.) *Slavery In New York*. New York, NY, The New Press, 2005.

Bethlehem Historical Association. *Records of the People of the Town of Bethlehem, Albany County, New York: 1698 – 1880*. Interlaken, NY: Heart of the Lakes Publishing, 1982.

Bethlehem History Committee; Brewer, Floyd I. (Sr. Ed.) *Bethlehem Revisited: A Bicentennial Story: 1793 – 1993*. Town of Bethlehem, NY: Bethlehem Bicentennial Commission, 1993.

Christman, Henry. *Tin Horns and Calico: A Decisive Episode in the Emergence of Democracy*. Cornwallville, NY: Hope Farm Press, 1978.

Clyne, Patricia Edwards. "Chapter 12: Climbing the Indian Ladder Trail," in *Hudson Valley Tales and Trails*. Woodstock, NY: The Overlook Press, 1990.

Dunn, Shirley W. and Bennett, Allison P. *Dutch Architecture Near Albany: the Polgreen Photographs*. Fleischmanns, NY: Purple Mountain Press, 1996.

Gregg, Arthur B. *Old Helleberg*. Guilderland Center, NY: Guilderland Historical Society, 1975.

Kobrin, David. *The Black Minority in Early New York*. Albany, NY: New York State American Revolution Bicentennial Commission, 1975.

New Scotland Historical Association. *New Scotland Township*. Charleston, SC: Arcadia Publishing, 2000.

Oliver, Merle. Interviewed by RoseAnne Fogarty, February 2011

CHAPTER 4

BEGINNINGS OF CONSERVATION:
DELMAR EXPERIMENTAL GAME FARM

Forest and wildlife conservation
are hereby declared to be
policies of the state.
For the purpose of carrying out such policies
the legislature may appropriate monies
for the acquisition by the state of land...
for the practice of
forest and wildlife conservation.

Constitution of the State of New York
Article XIV, Section 3.1.(1894)

In the 1830s Alexis de Toqueville had described Americans as "insensible to the wonders of inanimate nature" and charged that they valued nature's beauty only to the extent that it was also useful. But by mid-century, the runaway commercial and industrial development of the United States was provoking concern among thoughtful people. Writers like the New England Transcendentalists and artists like the Hudson River School reflected a new and growing sense that nature in and of itself is valuable.

At left, the Delmar Game Farm in its heyday. The Game Farm Superintendent lived in the Ackerman house to the far right. In the middle of the photograph are a brooder house and hatcheries. Behind them and running down to the pond is a pear orchard, a remnant of the Ackerman farm. (Five Rivers Archives)

The National Parks movement began with the 1872 establishment of Yellowstone, stalled for almost 20 years, and then gained momentum in the 1890s. By 1930, twenty national parks had been established, along with numerous national monuments. A coalition of the

31

influential and the eloquent, such as John Muir and Theodore Roosevelt, Virginia McClurg and Lucy Peabody, John D. Rockefeller, Stephen Mather, and Horace Albright built a groundswell of public support for saving the country's most unique and precious open spaces.

In New York, Article XIV of the state constitution, adopted in 1894, did not simply ensure the "forever wild" protection of the Adirondack Park. It also expressed a permanent commitment to open space and wildlife in New York. And not a moment too soon. Much of New York's woodlands had been clear cut by this time, with consequent loss of wildlife habitat. This, combined with over-hunting, was literally altering New York's landscape. Also at risk were the state's great watersheds, upon which its growing cities depended. As writer and entomologist Steve Nicholls expressed it,

> *The end of the nineteenth century was a low point for American wildlife. Ruthlessly exploited for profit, some spe-cies and subspecies had been wiped out entirely, and many others brought to the very brink of oblivion. (p. 133)*

Nicholls mentions the eastern bison, eastern elk, cougar, and passenger pigeons, exotic-sound-ing species but once common, he asserts, to upstate New York.

The first conservation work at Five Rivers grew out of precisely this crisis in species survival. It is interesting to note, however, that in this early "conservation" era, the pressure to save wildlife came from a sense of its usefulness—in this case, as game.

Establishing the Experimental Game Farm

The Delmar Experimental Game Farm, the fore-runner of Five Rivers, owes its beginning in 1933 to a dramatic decline in ruffed grouse. Wild turkeys, wood ducks, beaver, and even deer had almost disap-peared from the area, thanks to unregulated hunting

Area newspapers carried features about the photogenic Game Farm, fostering the public's interest. This 1939 feature in the old Knickerbocker News (now held in the archives of the Times Union) not only described the Farm's propagation techniques but also sent a clear "Visitors Welcome" message to the public. (Courtesy of the Times Union)

and loss of habitat. The ruffed grouse, or partridge, was a popular game bird because its erratic escape flight made it a challenging target, but it was also heavily hunted and even trapped year round during the Depression to supply the table.

Many of the most effective and committed early conservationists (like Theodore Roosevelt) were hunters and anglers, and the New York hunting community was upset by the loss of the popular game species. They pressured state government to address the problem.

Arthur A. Allen of Cornell University was already engaged in research to describe the full life cycle of the ruffed grouse. One of Allen's protégés, Gardiner Bump, was pursuing related research at a NYS Conservation Department site at Connecticut Hill near Ithaca. Bump moved to Delmar in 1929, planning to raise and study grouse. The Department's Commissioner at the time, Henry Morgenthau, Jr., told Bump "Find [a farm] that you want and we'll buy it."

Find one he did—a 113 acre farm in two parcels in Delmar and New Scotland owned by Edward and Catherine Ackerman. There were cornfields near the Vlomankill, a large wheat field in the area now surrounded by the North Loop Trail, and several orchards. In 1933 the Conservation Department bought the land for $10,000. The Ackerman Farm would become the core of the future Five Rivers, and was the first two of sixteen purchases that would bring together the 446 acres that are the Center today.

Shortly thereafter, the Civilian Conservation Corps, a key feature of Franklin Roosevelt's "New Deal," set up CCC Camp S-72 on the site to assist the state in developing the Game Farm. The CCC workers became an invaluable resource in the effort, constructing paths, roads, ponds, walls, and dams. They also modified existing buildings to create laboratories and

The damming of the Vlomankill by the Civilian Conservation Corps, described in Chapter 5, created the necessary habitat for breeding and wintering over various waterfowl. The building on the hill to the far right is the Wildlife Research Laboratory, built in 1941 and discussed in Chapter 7. (Five Rivers Archives)

temperature controlled breeding houses, and installed water and sewer systems connecting all the buildings. Chapter 5 will discuss the CCC Camp's work in detail.

Another feature of the growing enterprise at the site was a wildlife research laboratory established by Dr. Bump. The Lab will be further discussed in Chapter 7.

The Ruffed Grouse Breeding Program

The ruffed grouse proved to be a challenging species to work with. Vulnerable to many poultry diseases, their coops and the ground underneath had to be disinfected with flame guns. Brooder houses were built with wire mesh floors to keep the birds' feet off the ground. Two miles of surrounding fences were erected to keep out cats, dogs, skunks, and other predators.

By 1937, a thousand grouse were being hatched a year. Surplus birds were marked with a colored feather and sent to game refuges around the state and released.

Thanks to the Delmar Game Farm, the ruffed grouse became the subject of the first comprehensive study of a single species: *The Ruffed Grouse: Life History, Propagation, Management* published in 1947 by Gardiner Bump. Bump and his wife Janet, a self-trained wildlife pathologist, subsequently traveled to five continents studying game birds in the wild for the US Fish and Wildlife Service. (Five Rivers Archives)

The breeding process involved placing one male in a pen with two or three females. Every four days the eggs were placed in electrically heated incubators. Twenty-three days later, chicks hatched and received temporary leg bands coded for their parents. At three weeks they were given permanent wing bands that also noted the year of birth. Before release at maturity, they received another color-coded leg band indicating their generation.

At first, Game Farm researchers actually collected bee and fly larvae and ant eggs to feed the young grouse. Later they developed food and feeding methods that enabled them to feed the grouse much like chickens. Researchers learned to use overhead lights to control when the grouse would lay their eggs. Normal laying season was from April 1st to 15th, but with lights grouse could be induced to lay eggs in January, resulting in more and hardier birds for release in early summer.

The ruffed grouse experiment was abandoned in the early 1940s, mostly because the raised birds became too tame to be useful as game birds. Joe Dell, who worked at the site from 1941 to 1979, said the grouse "would walk up to people in the woods, taking all the fun out of it for hunters!"-- this from a notably skittish and elusive species.

Nonetheless, the thirteen years of research at the Delmar Game Farm and Connecticut Hill yielded the first complete study of the life history, physiology, pathology, and nesting habits of a wild species. Many scientific articles and a 900-page seminal book, *The Ruffed Grouse: Life History, Propagation, and Management* (of which Gardiner Bump was lead author), resulted.

Further Research: Species and Techniques

In 1937 the federal Pittman-Robinson Bill went into effect, enabling states to tax the sale of guns, ammunition, and sporting equipment using a formula based on the state's population and hunting license fees. This funding supported much of the research at Five Rivers, again making hunters a key source of conservation work.

The Game Farm developed a number of techniques to support bird species:
- Innovations in incubation, breeding, and rearing;
- More economical feeds and feeding methods;
- Development of the cannon net to trap birds that had been baited to a location;
- Invention of various chick soothing techniques for brooder houses.

Besides the ruffed grouse, several other species came under study at the Game Farm.

Ringneck Pheasant and Quail

The work done on grouse with artificial lights was also applied to pheasant and quail. Again, the species could be made to lay ahead of season. An incubator could hold over eighteen hundred pheasant eggs, for eventual release to the wild.

According to Game Farm superintendent Earl Holm, artificially speeding up the seasons allowed for the release of a larger and healthier population of birds that had longer to acclimate to

A Canada goose is freed. (Courtesy of Llwellyn Baker)

their environment upon release. This would also tend to eliminate breeding in July, when bird fertility was low and mortality high.

Records indicate that in 1937 alone, between sixty and seventy-five thousand pheasants were raised at the Game Farm. Eggs laid at other game farms in the state were also shipped in, candled over a light box to check for normal development, and then incubated. About eighty percent of the resulting chicks were shipped to sportsmen's clubs to raise and release after eight weeks. The remainder stayed at the Game Farm for twelve weeks, and then were shipped for direct release.

An "artificial mother" used at the Game Farm is an example of the challenges and creativity involved in working with wild species, such as the fragile and easily startled pheasant chicks. This particular device looked like a large canvas beach umbrella. It contained an ether cell and thermostat which activated an electric heater to keep the space under the umbrella at a constant 95 degrees. When chicks became cold they could dart through slits in the canvas to sleep in the artificial mother's warmth.

The Game Farm staff also used blue lights for their soothing effect, and filled corners with litter to prevent pile-ups of startled chicks in corners where many could be smothered. Thanks to this kind of problem-solving, six thousand chicks could be raised at a time in the Farm's two story brooder houses. At six weeks, chicks were placed in a twelve acre hardening field for six more weeks before release into the wild.

Ducks and Geese

Heron Pond and Beaver Pond, formed by CCC dams on the Vlomankill, made it possible for the Game Farm to experiment with waterfowl propagation. Staff studied mallards, black ducks, and Canada geese during the late 1930s and 1940s.

The pheasant hardening fields, where young birds were prepared for release. To the right is the Jones barn, and in the distance on the left is a brooder house; both still stand but are now painted brown. (Five Rivers Archives)

The brooder house still stands at the junction of the service road near the North Loop Trail, and is now designated Building 6. (Five Rivers Archives)

Mallards presented a problem similar to grouse: a tendency to become tame. Several small islands were built in the ponds as secure and isolated waterfowl nesting areas. Researchers would collect and incubate the eggs and then release young fowl at three, five, or seven weeks to observe results. Game Farm foreman Earl Holm, interviewed in 1937 by the *Knickerbocker News*, said,

> *Mallards released too late seem to have a tendency to find the nearest farmyard and stay there. We're trying to discover what age is best for release to leave the birds wild. Migration tendencies, nesting tendencies, and the birds' ability to care for themselves in the wild are studied. (6/20/1937, p.2)*

RINGNECKS IN RESERVE

THE ABC'S OF YOUR PHEASANT PRODUCTION LINE

BREEDING——*Six hen pheasants mate with one male in several thousand individual pens on New York's state game farms. The laying season lasts from April 1 to June 15, and the eggs are picked up daily. Over a quarter million are produced annually.*

INCUBATION——*More than 150,000 vigorous pheasant chicks hatched this year in modern incubators at two farms and thousands of additional eggs were incubated under domestic hens at others. Half the chicks were shipped to sportsmen's clubs for rearing.*

BROODING——*Efficient electric brooders and game farm attendants "mother" the baby chicks for five weeks in huge nursery buildings. Others are entrusted to the care of domestic hen foster-mothers on open range.*

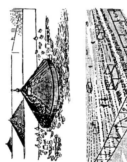

REARING——*At five weeks of age the chicks are transferred from nursery to big, open-top "hardening" yards, planted with corn, buckwheat and other natural foods. Birds are allowed to fly in and out until trapped and are well acclimated when time comes for their release.*

TRAPPING——*Birds in the hardening yards are baited into traps when 10 to 12 weeks of age. Despite normal losses from weather, predators, the death of weaklings, and escapes, from 60 to 80 per cent of all birds are trapped for shipment—and with a head start on life in the rough.*

SHIPPING——*Birds are placed in special fibre-board crates for shipment by train or truck to sportsmen's clubs for liberation. All State game is distributed through this cooperative arrangement and delays in release are greatly minimized.*

RESTOCKING——*Hardy, half-grown pheasants are released by game clubs on unposted land as soon as they are received. With the assistance of State game managers, club members select suitable environment to insure maximum survival.*

A publicity flyer published by the Game Farm. (Five Rivers Archives)

Wild ducks in the wintering pond, where a few chunks of ice are visible in the water. The sluice attached to the dam apparently helped to prevent the water from freezing, enabling the ducks to stay longer. (Five Rivers Archives)

In another project, researchers cross-bred native black ducks with a low breeding rate with East Indian black ducks that were prolific breeders. The resulting so-called Flanders Duck was then rebred with native black ducks to encourage a higher breeding rate in the native species.

Game Farms in the Environmental Continuum

The noted environmental writer Aldo Leopold had worked for the US Forest Service and was also a hunter. Perhaps due to these experiences, his writing is as much about human perception of nature as it is about nature itself. He writes of the reality that nature is viewed from diverse perspectives-- wilderness for recreation, for science, and for wildlife itself-- and of the need to educate the human perspective on nature.

Although game farms seem an anomaly in the light of today's environmental thinking, they played a seminal role in keeping the importance of wildlife in the public eye during a transitional era. By emphasizing the usefulness of nature and its wild species, they helped to protect those species. They also helped foster a growing consensus in support of environmental preservation. As Aldo Leopold said in concluding his 1949 classic, *A Sand County Almanac,*

It would appear... that the rudimentary grades of outdoor recreation consume their resource-base; the higher grades, at least to a degree, create their own satisfactions with little or no attrition of land or life....Recreational development [therefore] is a job not of building roads into lovely country, but of building receptivity into the still unlovely human mind. (pp. 294-5)

Chapter 4 Resources

Baker, Llewelyn (Earl). Correspondence with Nancy Payne,

Budliger, Robert. Review of "Five Rivers History." Delmar, NY, Five Rivers Archives: January 2012.

Bump, Gardiner. *Pheasant Rearing.* Delmar, NY: Five Rivers Archives, undated.

Constitution of the State of New York, Article XVI

Dell, Joe. Interview by Dan Ruge. Delmar, NY: Fiver Rivers Archives, June 8, 1993

Duncan, Dayton and Burns, Ken. *The National Parks: America's Best Idea—An Illustrated History.* New York: Alfred A Knopf, 2009

The Knickerbocker News, Albany, NY, Sunday, June 30, 1937, (Section 1, p. 2?). *State Game Farm at Delmar Speeds Wild Bird Tests to Supply Hunters in Fall with Pheasants and Ducks.*

The Knickerbocker News, Albany, NY, Monday, April 17, 1939, (Section 2, p. 1). *A Game Crop is a Community Asset: New York State Experimental Game Farm.*

Leopold, Aldo. *A Sand County Almanac.* New York: Ballantine Books, 1970.

Nicholls, Steve. Paradise Found: Nature in America at the Time of Discovery. Chicago, IL: University of Chicago Press, 2009

CHAPTER 5

THE CIVILIAN CONSERVATION CORPS

In his 1936 report summarizing the CCC's first two years,
Director Robert Fechner described the corps as giving "jobs to
hundreds of thousands of discouraged and undernourished young men,
idle through no fault of their own,
to build up these young men physically and spiritually
and to start the nation on a sound conservation program
which would conserve and expand our timber resources,
increase recreational opportunities and
reduce the annual toll taken by
disease, pests, soil erosion, and floods."

David Stradling
The Nature of New York

From November 7, 1933 to September 29, 1936, a Civilian Conservation Corps Camp-- Company Ruffed Grouse, Camp S-72-- was in existence in Delmar and New Scotland on the site of the recently formed Delmar Experimental Game Farm. The CCC in New York is a fascinating example of the conservation perspective of the early 20ᵗʰ Century.

Franklin Delano Roosevelt is not generally identified in popular thinking as a conservationist, but in fact he was a worthy successor to his cousin Theodore in that respect. In 1911, when he was elected to the New York State Senate, he eagerly took the chairmanship of the Forest, Fish, and Game Committee. In the years that followed he became convinced of the importance of renewing New York's

41

This photo of the CCC encampment shows the barracks in the foreground, with the dining hall and workshops behind them. The only buildings in this picture that remain standing are the two farthest, now Operation/Maintenance Building No. 3 (left) and Goose Lodge Building No. 4 (right). The crab-apple orchard behind them, planted as an experiment in providing winter forage for birds, still flourishes. (Five Rivers Archives)

rural landscape, both through farm assistance and through reforestation. As Governor of New York in the late 1920's he became convinced of the need to preserve open spaces, and even advocated the return of populations to the countryside, to reduce the size of the cities that became a trap for hopeless multitudes during the depression.

Environmental historian David Stradling notes that Governor Roosevelt's "active governance in New York State, which included hiring ten thousand men to work in forestry in 1932, helped him gain the Democratic presidential nomination and ensured his victory in November." It was only natural for FDR to then seek to repeat that success with a national corps, which he did in 1933. Many young men jumped at the chance to earn a steady paycheck of thirty dollars a month, twenty-five dollars of which was automatically sent home to provide family support. Workers enlisted for six months, after which they could reenlist. The CCC promised food, lodging, and the chance to learn skills and build work experience.

Four federal agencies collaborated in establishing the CCC. The Department of Labor selected unemployed, unmarried young men between the ages of eighteen and twenty-five, from needy families, for enrollment. The U.S. Army enrolled them, formed them into companies, and arranged for the provision of food, clothing, and equipment. Army regulars or reservists—captains, lieutenants, and sergeants-- oversaw the regimented camp life of the workers. The Departments of Agriculture and the Interior designated the work sites and directed the work to be done.

One has to respect a four-agency collaboration that was able to establish so many facilities so quickly, almost on a wartime basis. Plans for the first two camps in New York were initiated less than two months after Roosevelt took office, and by 1935 New York's Conservation Department was supervising sixty-seven camps. In that year alone CCC workers planted over thirty-seven million trees in New York, in the process reforesting thirty-two thousand acres.

According to Craig Thompson, Five Rivers Center Director, every state in the nation participated in the CCC, but New York's program was the largest. Between 1933 and 1942, a total of 208 CCC encampments were established in New York.

Life in the CCC at the Delmar Experimental Game Farm

The CCC Company at Delmar was named "Ruffed Grouse" for the work being done at the Game Farm, which bred, raised, and released ruffed grouse for hunters. The camp consisted of roughly 200 men, with five officers and seven foremen. The enlistees came from all walks of life, from dropouts and drifters to high school and college graduates. The foremen were World War I veterans or experienced woodsmen. There were also skilled craftsmen who instructed the enlistees in carpentry, masonry, electrical work, and blacksmithing.

The dozen or so buildings included five barracks, each containing forty single beds. There was an officers' quarters, a post exchange, a recreation building, a six-bed infirmary, a mess hall, a blacksmith's shop, a mechanical shop, a woodworking shop, a supply building, a washroom and shower building, and a large latrine. There was also a garage for the four or five state trucks used at the camp.

The small recreation building served as the main gathering place, with a snack bar and a ping pong table. The mess hall could hold 125 men. The food was good, the men always hungry, and their plates nearly always clean by meal's end.

Conditions were not always ideal. "You never got a pair of shoes that fit you," recalled one worker, "All of our clothes were from World War I." The living quarters were Spartan, open-interior barracks with lines of beds. Three large pot-bellied stoves provided the only heat in each barracks, leaving them too cold for much of the year. The stoves burned soft coal and "you could taste it in your mouth when you woke up," said a worker.

Company 270, Camp S-72, CCC, Delmar, N. Y.

The CCC barracks. (Five Rivers Archives)

Inside a barracks at Camp Ruffed Grouse. Note the coal-burning stove on the right. (Five Rivers Archives)

The Daily Routine

Life in the camp was regimented, in a somewhat relaxed military style. The men were awakened at 6:30 A.M. by a bugler. After washing, shaving, dressing, and making their beds, men reported to the mess hall for breakfast. They then returned to their barracks to wait for the call to assembly, at which time they lined up for the flag raising and to receive their daily work assignments.

Those assigned near the camp ate lunch in the mess hall; those farther away were served from a chow wagon. Work finished at 4:30 P.M., when all returned to camp to clean up and report for supper. Afterwards a CCC truck would carry any discarded food and other refuse to the Albany Dump. Albert Lanoue, an enrollee who drove the truck, recalled that times were so difficult that when he backed up his truck at the dump, even before the tires stopped moving, people would jump on the truck to grab leftover food.

Albert J. Lanoue
CCC Camp Delmar, NY
ca. 1936

Albert Lanoue, a driver and auto maintenance worker for the CCC camp. (Five Rivers Archives)

After assembling for TAPS and flag lowering after dinner, the men had the rest of the day to do as they liked. "Lights out" was at 9:00 P.M., with curfew at midnight. Worried about fire, the officer of the day would check all stoves around 9:30. If a red glow remained in the bottom of a stove he would turn on the light and roust all forty men out of their beds. Two of them were then required empty the embers out of the stove with a shovel and bucket, take them outdoors, and douse them with water.

Not surprisingly, the men were cold all night. One enrollee, Art Smith, recalled "I slept three beds away from the stove. When I awoke in the morning, I'd take my clothes from the hook by my bed and sometimes have to shake off snow, after which I slid them under the covers to warm them." He also remembered the wind blowing so hard at times during the winter that the snow came up through the floorboards and he would awake to find a small snowdrift on his feet.

Payday came at the end of each month. The officer of the day would go to the bank in Delmar to pick up the men's payroll. When he returned, recalled Bert Poland, he would draw his gun before carrying the money—all silver dollars—into the mess hall where the men were paid. One day, Poland said, the officer forgot his gun so he picked up a brick to protect the payroll instead!

According to enrollee Llewellyn Baker, sometimes camp routine was broken by unusual events. "A cup of gasoline was added to the mop water to scrub down the barracks floor to keep the dust down," as Baker told the tale.

When mopping was finished the leftover water was dumped down the service latrine. One day the fire alarm sounded and everyone dropped their shovels and ran for the camp. When we got there, the latrine was on fire and there were four men blown halfway through the canvas top with their legs and bare behinds scorched. It seems there were three men sitting on the latrine when a fourth man came in, sat down, and lit cigarette and threw the match down the next hole. We got the fire out and took the men to the infirmary where the doctor kept them for a week. The building was damaged very little apart from the canvas roof.

Although this makes an entertaining story, former Fiver Rivers Center Director Bob Budliger insists that it is entirely apocryphal—"a military barracks legend that has been told and retold (I heard it first at Ft. Carson, CO, in the 50s.)" Llewellyn Baker earned the nickname "Tarzan" for

his interest in all manner of wildlife. After his CCC years he was hired at the Game Farm, and served as acting superintendent during World War II.

Besides telling tall tales, the men enjoyed played softball for recreation, or hitchhiked to Delmar or Albany for a movie. Once a week a truck went to town, and sometimes camp members would be trucked to Lincoln Park in Albany for a day of lunch, softball, and horseshoes. A veteran of the CCC at Delmar affirmed that most of the men got along well, despite their varied backgrounds and life experiences.

Llewellyn Baker, a member of the CCC camp, became known as "Tarzan" because of his interest in all wildlife. When the CCC camp closed he was hired at the Game Farm, eventually serving as Assistant Game Farm Foreman until 1963. In charge of the incubators, he estimated that he hatched over half a million eggs during his service. (Five Rivers Archives)

Contributions of the CCC

The Corps' work was not confined to the Delmar Experimental Game Farm property. Workers were also trucked to a number of sites throughout the Capital Region, such as East Berne, where they planted trees. At the Game Farm, the CCC enrollees built roads and paths, walls and dams, ponds, barracks, and sixteen buildings to support the game bird breeding effort, as well as laying sewage and water lines. In addition, four or five men were assigned specifically to Game Farm duty, including feeding the birds and cleaning their shelters.

One of the biggest jobs at the Game Farm was the construction of three dams on the Vlomankill. These created two ponds for breeding black and mallard ducks, and a third and larger impoundment to provide water to pump to the pheasant pens in the north fields. One dam was 350 feet long, seventy to eighty feet wide, eighteen feet high, and flooded fifteen acres of land. All the excavation and fill was done by hand by the CCC workers.

CCC enrollees working on the dam between Heron and Beaver ponds. (Courtesy of the Times Union)

Another large job involved creating two series of ponds as feeding areas for young birds just out of the incubators, three ponds in one group and four in the other. The men also fenced the entire farm against predators such as foxes, weasels, skunks, and house cats (apparently the worst offenders) that might attack the birds.

The massive stone blocks in the dams and walls around Five Rivers were limestone blocks from the Erie Canal. The canal was unpopular with the residents along its banks because of the stench of the mule manure constantly being replenished along the towpaths. The moment traffic on the canal ceased, there was a demand to demolish it. The stones eventually found their way to many public and private construction project sites, including Five Rivers.

The CCC men nicknamed the program "Colossal College of Calluses," a reference to the long days of hard work. Some outsiders (perhaps parents who didn't appreciate enrollees' attention to

Above left: The spillway between Heron and Beaver Ponds under CCC construction (facing West). In addition, the CCC workers also built service roads, paths, sewage and water lines, and brooder houses. They also fenced the entire Game Farm against predators. (Courtesy of the Times Union)

Above right: The finished spillway between the ponds, showing the massive stone blocks recycled from the Erie Canal. (Five Rivers Archives)

More CCC stonework using stone blocks salvaged from the Erie Canal. (Photo by RA Fogarty)

their daughters) preferred "Canvas Covered Convicts." Some CCC workers did date local young women, and a number married and settled down in the area. A few men were hired after their CCC service to work at the Game Farm, including Bert Poland and Llewellyn "Tarzan" Baker.

On September 29, 1936, with the Delmar Experimental Game Farm well established, Company Ruffed Grouse moved on to Whitney Point, NY, to work on US Army Corps of Engineers projects.

Taking Stock of the CCC's Contributions

The Civilian Conservation Corps reflected the environmental values of the early 20th Century. Its primary purpose, of course, was to put men to work, and the goal of that work was to preserve and enhance nature for human benefit. Thus, for example, reforestation was done largely with fast-growing evergreens which increased the timber supply but also changed the character of the state's preexisting mixed hardwood forests.

Five Rivers Center Director Craig Thompson put these efforts in context in an article published in the February 2008 issue of *New York State Conservationist*.

> *The great Depression was about much more than economic chaos.... It was a time of national environmental crisis as well. Forest fires were frequent and often severe, and fire-fighting capability was limited. Forest pests and diseases were out of control. Imprudent plowing of grasslands, overgrazing of public lands, over-cutting of forest lands, and soil exhaustion had led to severe erosion and stream siltation throughout the U.S. Fish and wildlife stocks were in decline. Many areas were ravaged by flooding. And the increasing availability of automobiles put tremendous pressure on already overburdened parks and fish and wildlife resources. (p. 32)*

Today some critics may question the decision to construct Skyline Drive through Shenandoah National Park, or some of the many other scenic roads built by the CCC. However, in building those roads to give people access to the nation's natural wonders, the Corps was building a constituency for environmental preservation itself, a very necessary step in the evolution of public thinking. Millions of American and foreign tourists have enjoyed the fruits of the CCC workers labors, including the Pacific Crest Trail, the Appalachian Trail, 800 state parks and 52,000 acres of campground. In the process, public opinion evolved. What deTocqueville had described in the 1830s as American indifference to nature was becoming, a century later, a growing appreciation of our natural treasures.

The CCC was remembered in this 1999 article in the Daily Gazette. Veterans of the corps (l. to r.) Carlton Morby, Don Dietz, and John Steele reminisced about the heavy work ("no chain saws") , the meals ("a lot of apple butter"), and the pay, $30 a month of which the enrollees were encouraged to send home $25. "You were young," said Steele. "It was a great, great experience." (Courtesy of the Daily Gazette)

Chapter 5 Resources

Baker, George. Interview by Dan Ruge. Albany, NY: Five Rivers Archives. June 23, 1993.

Baker, Llewellyn. Personal Writings. Albany, NY: Five Rivers Archives, undated.

Baldridge, Kenneth W. *The Civilian Conservation Corps;* Utah History Encyclopedia. July 1, 2006. http://www.media.utah.edu/UHE/c/CIVCONCOR.html

_____. *Civilian Conservation Corps.* Maryland Department of Natural Resources. June 25, 2006. http://www.dnr.state.md.us/publiclands/cchistory.html

Dell, Joe. Interview by Dan Ruge. Albany, NY: Five Rivers Archives, June 8, 1993

Dietz, Donald. *Five Rivers Environmental Education Center and the CCCs*, June 25, 2006. http://www.geocities.com/cchistory/270.html

Duncan, Dayton and Burns, Ken. *The National Parks: America's Best Idea.* New York: Alfred A. Knopf, 2009.

Stradling, David. *The Nature of New York: An Environmental History of the Empire State.* Ithaca, NY: Cornell University Press, 2010.

Thompson, Craig. "Force for Nature: 75 Years Later: The Legacy of the Civilian Conservation Corps," *New York State Conservationist,* February 2008, pp. 30-36.

Wilkin, Jeff. Forgotten Contribution: Young men in Civilian Conservation Corps toiled long and hard beautifying American during the Great Depression. *The Daily Gazette,* Tuesday, Oct. 2, 1999, p. D1.

Clint Bishop represents a time when knowledge still outweighed college degrees, and a person could become a recognized expert through sheer hard work and love of his subject. (Five Rivers Archives)

CHAPTER 6

THE DELMAR "ZOO"

If the first frontier was explored by the acquisitive Lewis and Clark,
the second frontier was romanticized by Teddy Roosevelt;
if the first frontier was the real Davy Crockett's,
the second frontier peaked with Disney's Davy.
If the first frontier was a time of struggle,
the second frontier was a time of taking stock, of celebration.
It brought a new politics of preservation,
an immersion of Americans in the domesticated and romanticized
fields and woods and streams around them.

Richard Louv
Last Child in the Woods

Paradoxically, the thing that may have contributed most to the evolution of the Delmar Game Farm into Five Rivers as a continuing base for the study of nature was a program that emerged informally and unofficially, under the radar of government legislation. It was the spontaneous result of one couple's delight in and devotion to wildlife. It was the "Delmar Zoo" at the Delmar Experimental Game Farm that won the hearts of a generation of community members and their children, making it their special place.

Animal Rehabilitation, Then and Now

Today's nature ethic urges us, "If you care, leave them there." Wild birds and animals, sometimes even injured ones, have the best chance of surviving, reproducing, and living out healthy

lives in their natural environments, or so we now believe. Scions of endangered species are painstakingly reintroduced to their native habitats, and the goal is always to create a healthy population that will survive and thrive without further human intervention. Environmentalists of today also place a high value on species diversity, and want to see a healthy balance of many coexisting plant and animal species, not just a few that have an obvious value from a human viewpoint.

However, many citizens had to be slowly brought to a point where they could appreciate nature for itself, not simply for its value as source of game animals, lumber, and edible plants. Parents and grandparents of the 1950's and 60's may first have enjoyed a passion for the wild as they saw their children's delight at the Central Park Zoo, the Brooklyn Botanical Garden, or the Catskill Game Farm. According to former Five Rivers Director Bob Budliger, a number of other Conservation Department facilities and state parks had live animal displays during this period, before the appearance of modern animal care standards and the certification of animal rehabilitators.

The Delmar Zoo

Most local citizens became aware of the Delmar Experimental Game Farm through the creation of the Delmar Zoo. Conservation aide Clinton Bishop and his wife Frances lived near the railroad crossing on New Scotland Road South, where they bred terriers and also kept a bustling menagerie of wildlife. Clint's natural affinity for wildlife was put to good use with his care of the game birds at the Game Farm, but he also tended to be a magnet for injured birds and animals. According to a coworker, "Clint was always taking in something new to nurse back to health."

The educational emphasis was there from the beginning, as reflected in this welcome sign: "We hope you like this little exhibit. We're trying to keep it clean, interesting, and truly educational." (Five Rivers Archives)

A few animals: a bobcat, a grey fox, and a raccoon, were kept at the zoo to inform studies of how predators leave their prey after a kill. Injured animals were sometimes brought to the Bishops for rehabilitation, and some could not be returned to the wild, like this weasel. As the collection grew, so did public interest (just as today the barred owl, Aries, is the first stop for most visitors to the Center building.) (Five Rivers Archives)

"Taking his show on the road," Clint Bishop attempted to display animals in a large and naturalistic enclosure. Here is an albino deer that he sometimes took to sportsmen's conventions in the enclosure he constructed. (Five Rivers Archives)

In 1948, the zoo began to take shape as Clint began to display the many animals he was caretaking. Eventually it consisted of a number of cages as well as a deer pen and a small penned in pond for waterfowl. Among the more popular animals over the years were a trio of bear cubs, dubbed Rosy, Posy, and Dosy, housed in the structure near the Five Rivers parking lot that is still called "The Bear Pen." Other popular animals included an albino skunk and a talking crow named Jimmy.

Inevitably, people came not only to see the animals on display but also to bring injured animals they had found, for care. A coworker reported that "[Clint] estimated that, at one time or another, he had handled every mammal native to New York State."

Besides the zoo, Bishop developed traveling educational exhibits which he took to fairs, sportsmen's shows, and conventions around the state. He used a twenty by thirty foot semi-circular cage to display song birds, pheasants, wild turkeys, and deer, lining the cage with red pine, driftwood, and greenery to maintain a natural feeling.

Change and Continuity

Game farms in New York began to close in the late 1960s. The thinking behind breeding and stocking game animals had changed. Albert Hall, then Director of New York State's Division of

Fish and Wildlife, explained that:

"[It was] now recognized that the land has a specific carrying capacity for all wildlife and the most effective means of increasing wildlife population is not by artificially stocking it but by improving the habitat required by the species in question. Game refuges, once held to be essential in management, are now regarded as unessential except for migratory birds."

Since the Delmar Zoo had been pieced together as a side project, it never met safety standards for animals or visitors. A consultant gave the Conservation Department an estimate of the investment needed to bring it up to standards, but the cost ($200,000) was considered prohibitive. There had also been a troubling incident in autumn of 1968, in which four deer at the game farm were sadistically killed during the night. Two young men were arrested and charged. Unfortunately, one inevitable conclusion could be drawn from the incident: penned animals are vulnerable animals.

As people are now discovering, fed animals become tame animals and their tameness then makes them at jeopardy in the wild and a nuisance in civilization. The conservation ethic has now become "If you care, leave them there." (Five Rivers Archives)

With changes in the organization of the Conservation Department and changes in conservation philosophy, the decision was made in 1971 to close the Game Farm and its zoo. But the Delmar Zoo by 1971 had a passionate constituency. At that point it housed twenty mammals including opossum, porcupine, woodchuck, coyote, black bear, fox, snowshoe hare, skunk, raccoon, and deer, along with twenty-five birds including hawks, owls, game birds, and waterfowl. These were being visited by thousands of children each year, in family groups and school classes.

Community protest at the closing of the Game Farm and especially the Delmar Zoo reached such a pitch that it attracted the attention of some powerful advocates. A later chapter will explain how the waning concept of a wildlife zoo was able to morph into the new ideal of an environmental education center.

The Bishops were heard from again, as well. In 1995 a portion of the Bishop property was put up for sale. Thanks to the generous donations of its members, the Friends of Five Rivers purchase seventeen acres which it held until the state was able to buy it, thus giving Five Rivers a permanent and tangible link to the animal lover who introduced thousands of people to wildlife.

The strong identification of local people with their " Zoo" would pay off twenty years later, when the Delmar Game Farm was being closed. Chapters 8 and 9 tell that story. (Five Rivers Archives)

Chapter 6 Resources

Armstrong, Shirley. "Delmar Game Farm Planning 'Native Setting' for Stock. *Times Union,* Albany, NY, August 26, 1970

Budliger, Robert. Review of "Five Rivers History." January 2012.

Gallman, Norman J. "Delmar Game Farm Is Exciting Wildlife 'Orphanage'." *Union Star*, December 15, 1962.

O'Connor, Grace. "He Talks of His Animals with Affection." *Times Union*, February 9, 1970.

Pankin, Elle. "Game Farm Future Debated as Delmar "Zoo" Is Closed," *Times Union*, Albany, NY, Sunday, October 10, 1971, Feature Section, p.1.

"2 Charged in Killing of Deer." *Knickerbocker News*. Albany, Tuesday, Dec. 3, 1968.

Biologists from the Wildlife Research Center test radio tracking gear in 1970. (Five Rivers Archives)

CHAPTER 7

THE WILDLIFE RESEARCH CENTER

Many a sportsman, as he proudly exhibits his trophies of the hunt,
does not realize... that behind his prowess lies
the helping hand of conservationists....
The Wildlife Research Center at Delmar, NY, is typical
of conservation laboratories throughout the country,
where teams of conservationists, zoologists, and botanists
work out such problems as deer growth;
paths and tendencies of migratory game birds;
the causes of wildlife diseases and their remedies.
They attempt to discover a pattern of behavior in animals...
observations...which, if accurate, establish
a certain measure of scientific control....

People and Places Magazine
November 1956

Environmental science was not a highly visible or recognized field in the 1950s, as the quotation above makes clear. The college and graduate programs in environmental studies, the research labs with government and private funding for environmental research, the networks for data collection on myriad species: all were in the future.

Five Rivers' first wildlife laboratory was a tiny one-room affair containing the bare essentials of a lab. This was in 1933, and in these cramped quarters research, experiments, autopsies, and operations were carried out.

Beginnings

The original "laboratory," if it could be called that, was converted in a few years to a brooder house for ruffed grouse. William Severinghaus, who had worked during summers at the Conservation Department's Connecticut Hill facility, came to Delmar in 1938. The Conservation Department then turned over the old Civilian Conservation Corps infirmary to the Wildlife Research Lab. The infirmary had the advantage of already having some laboratory facilities, as well as considerably more space.

The Lab's first research work was divided into components, each tied to a specific animal species or grouping: deer, pheasants, grouse, quail, cottontail rabbits and varying hares, mallards, black ducks, and furbearers like muskrats. The point of each study was to collect life history on the species, to develop large scale management techniques, and to estimate their cost.

Other research at the Lab examined the extent of deer damage and explored suitable control strategies (research that many residents of the Five Rivers area today would no doubt endorse!) The Research Lab also investigated predator-prey relationships, wildlife diseases and parasites, and feeding habits, and carried out biometric analyses of wildlife data.

The Wildlife Research Center came into formal existence in 1938 as a necessary adjunct to the Game Farm, which had been studying incubation, nutrition, rearing, and pathology of game species from its inception. (Five Rivers Archives)

Funding

As the Wildlife Research Lab was getting up and running, federal and state attention to environmental issues was increasing. In 1937, Congress had enacted the Federal Aid in Wildlife Restoration Act (known as the Pittman-Robertson Act.) Under the Act, federal and state governments would work to "not only preserve our present-day limited supply of wildlife, but to restore it to some semblance of its former abundance."

As noted in Chapter 4, wildlife research and restoration was to be funded under the Act largely through excise taxes on the sale of sporting equipment, arms, and ammunition. The principle was that money taken in from sportsmen's license fees and excise taxes should be spent to maintain the species they hunted. New York enacted laws prohibiting the diversion of licensing fees to any purpose other than conservation. This then qualified New York to receive federal monies under the Pittman-Robertson Act.

Growing Facilities, Staff, and Challenges

In late 1938, three young scientists were added to the staff of the Wildlife Research Lab. E.L. Cheatum and Frans C. Goble were biologists and wildlife pathologists; John C. Jones was a food habits investigator. Dr. Goble, a state biologist, worked primarily on pheasants, hares, and other species that were raised at the game farm but were not part of the federally funded program. Dr. Cheatum, whose position was federally funded, worked primarily on the physiology, growth, and survival of white-tailed deer.

In 1941, a new Wildlife Research Laboratory building was completed above Heron Pond. It featured two spacious refrigerators that could hold fifty or more deer carcasses, and also had a room equipped to preserve small game for experimental purposes.

Approximately 3000 wildlife specimens were sent to the lab each year during the 1940s. Many came from hunters and game farms but, in addition, every wild animal found dead by New York State conservation officers, whether in the woods or along the highway, was sent to the Delmar lab to be "posted." This required post-mortem exam provided the lab with many specimens for study.

Drs. Cheatum and Goble performed autopsies on each specimen to determine cause of death and to study any parasites and diseases. When their work was done, animal stomachs were given to Dr. Jones, who studied wildlife diets and feeding habits.

Deer Research

"Every day a fresh deer carcass was brought to us from somewhere in the state by conservation officers or sportsmen," recalled Joe Dell, a wildlife biologist employed by the lab from 1941 to 1979.

From these carcasses we determined age, and we needed other reproductive indicators. At that time, and still today, we used the lower jaw bone—that's a very good indicator. Bill Severinghaus, along with Jack Tanck, developed the method for aging deer and it's still used internationally today.

The carcasses would be brought in every day of the year, even in midsummer with the pall of heat which meant that there were flies and maggots and, of course, the carcass was bloated. Some deer carcasses were two or three, even four days old. They'd be pulled off the parcel post truck and dumped in the shed. First I had to get the gas out of the stomach or abdomen. I got pretty proficient at knife throwing so that I could slit it open and let the gas escape before having to approach the carcass. We then removed the canon bone from the front leg, and took the jaw bone for study.

The work of the Delmar lab proved to be very important to deer management programs throughout the country. The lab developed techniques to age deer and ways to determine their reproductive rates. It also studied the relationship between food and foraging range, on the one hand, and

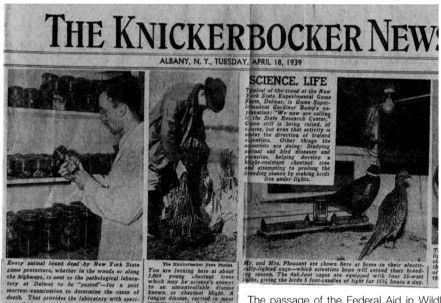

The passage of the Federal Aid in Wildlife Restoration Act (the Pittman-Robertson Act) in 1938 enabled federally funded projects. According to this Knickerbocker News article, by 1939 the lab was studying such diverse topics as animal and bird diseases and parasites, developing blight resistant chestnut trees, and prolonging the bird breeding season with the use of artificial light. (Courtesy of the Times Union)

deer life span and reproductive success, on the other. All this significantly improved understanding of deer population dynamics.

Wildlife Diseases and Toxins

The Wildlife Pathology Unit of the Wildife Research Laboratory has been conducting pioneering research since its inception in the late 1930s. Early work focused on the nutritional requirements of deer and the impact of cold temperatures and snowy conditions on deer populations. In the 1940s and 50s, the lab also studied deer and waterfowl parasites and the impact of ingesting lead shotgun pellets on waterfowl and pheasant mortality.

During the 1960s, research was conducted on rabies in foxes and skunks. In the 1970s, the Wildlife Pathology Unit improved the "cementum annuli" method for reading rings on the teeth of foxes, raccoons, and bears, and also studied furbearer diseases intensively.

By 1969, when a new facility was added to the 1941 structure, the Lab had ongoing research programs in the following areas: wildlife pathology, waterfowl, upland game bird, small mammals, wildlife food and cover, big game, game hunting take, and rabies.

In the 1940s every animal found dead by NYS Conservation Officers was sent to the Lab to be posted. This added up to about 3000 animals per year, including hundreds of deer carcasses. (Five Rivers Archives)

During the 1970s and 80s the lab diagnosed many bird deaths as caused by insecticides, including DDT, Diazinon, Oftano, and Dursban. The Delmar wildlife pathologist at the time, Ward Stone, was a principal expert used by the Environmental Protection Agency at the historic 1987 hearing that resulted in the ban on Diazinon use on golf courses and sod farms.

(It is worth noting here that although the DEC's Bureau of Wildlife would have preferred to keep the Game farm site for research only, Stone was an advocate for the establishment of an environmental education center, and served on the board of Five Rivers Ltd.)

Investigation of contaminant issues continued in

the late 1980s when the Lab studied PCB contamination in the St. Lawrence River. Working with the Mohawk Nation, the Lab discovered and quantified PCB sources near the river at industrial plants owned by General Motors and Reynolds Metals. Further pollution studies were conducted in the 1990s at landfills, construction debris dumps, and incinerators.

Protecting the Future of All Species

Moving on into the 21ˢᵗ Century, the Lab has been involved in the study of numerous disease outbreaks and environmental poisonings, with growing awareness of the total food chain and ecosystem. A case in point was the unexpected die-off of loons and other migratory birds on the Great Lakes in 1999. This was found to be directly linked to an explosion in invasive mussels that produced Type E botulism toxin. It was determined that the toxin sank to the bottom of the lakes where small fish, particularly round gobies, would feed. Loons and other birds would then feed on the fish carrying the deadly toxin. In 2002 twenty-five thousand dead birds were found on Lake Erie alone, and another outbreak occurred in 2006.

The new century also brought the West Nile Virus, in which mosquitoes were vectors transmitting the disease from crows to

NEW YORK STATE CONSERVATION DEPARTMENT

Wildlife Research Laboratory

Delmar, New York

DEDICATION
October 22, 1969

DIVISION OF FISH AND WILDLIFE

State of New York
Nelson A. Rockefeller, Governor

Conservation Department
R. Stewart Kilborne, Commissioner

66

humans. The Lab helped to pinpoint the locations and spread of the disease through testing of dead crows. The Wildlife Research Center and its Wildlife Pathology Unit continue to play an important role in surveillance of threats to our wildlife and environment.

A new laboratory building was opened in 1969, not long before the decision was made to close the Game Farm. The emphasis had shifted from "farming" game to studying and preserving habitat. (Five Rivers Archives)

Chapter 7 Resources

Alsheimer, Charles J. "Forty Years of Deer Research," *Deer and Deer Hunting*. February 1983,: 33-37.

Budliger, Robert. *Review of "Five Rivers History."* January 2012

Cartledge, Jerry. "Delmar Lab Is Center of Huge Wildlife Research Program," *Times Union*, Albany, NY, Sunday, March 1, 1959 (Section E, pp. 4 and 6.)

Dell, Joe. Interview by Dan Ruge, Albany NY: Five Rivers Archives, June 8, 1993.

Grondahl, Paul. "Loons' Water Turns Deadly," *Times Union*. October 27, 2006, (Section A, pp. 1 and 8.)

"Help for the Hunter," *People and Places Magazine,* November 1956: 8-10.

Peterson, Ray. "Wildlife 'lab' at Delmar Ready—to Minute Detail; To Be Dedicated Friday," *The Knickerbocker News,* Albany, NY, Wednesday, Sept. 24, 1941, (Section A, p. 14)

"Science, Life." *The Knickerbocker News*, Albany, NY, Tuesday, April 18, 1939, (Second section, p. 1)

Five Rivers as it appeared at its inception. (Five Rivers Archives)

CHAPTER 8

CONSERVATION COMES OF AGE:

FIVE RIVERS ENVIRONMENTAL EDUCATION CENTER

Located about three miles south of Delmar, NY,
is the former Delmar Game Farm,
owned and operated by the Department from 1933 until 1971
for the propagation of game birds and animals....
With the phasing out of the game propagation program at Delmar
much of the land and some of the building
have become available for other uses.
We feel that the Delmar Game Farm site can be adapted for use
as an environmental education center.

"Capitol Area Environmental
Education Center at Delmar (proposed)"
White paper published in Fall of 1971

The late 1960s and early 1970s are often regarded as a time of turmoil. Values were being reexamined across the board and environmentalism, like race relations and the Vietnam War, was a focus of attention. Game farms throughout New York were being closed for a variety of reasons. Expense was a factor as well as economies of scale, but the major reason was the gradual change in philosophy regarding wild species and their environments. No longer was the goal to breed species in captivity and then release them. Environmental research was now focusing on habitats, carrying capacity, the value of diversity of species and habitats, and the interaction of myriad species within each habitat.

The Environmental Education Center Concept

As game farms closed, the idea of the "nature center" enjoyed a boom, strongly influenced by the National Audubon Society, which ran an active Nature Center Planning Division. When the Rogers Game Farm in Sherburne, NY, closed down in the mid-1960s, the community was concerned about loss of jobs and open recreational space. National Audubon Society supported a study to determine how to best meet the community's need. In 1966, the New York Conservation Department established the Rogers Conservation Education Center. It also initiated a plan, never fully implemented, to establish environmental education centers in each region of the state, using surplus state land or former wildlife management areas.

In 1970, the Conservation Department was reorganized and renamed. Henceforth it would be the New York State Department of Environmental Conservation (DEC), and the (eventually) four education centers would be called environmental education centers.

When the Delmar Game Farm and "Zoo" were threatened with closure, local activitists petitioned the state to maintain them, but to no avail. They were closed in 1971. However, the site fit well with the DEC plan for environmental education centers, which National Audubon Society also supported. The potential for a citizen-government partnership became apparent.

Shortly thereafter, with encouragement from DEC, a small group of citizens formed "Five Rivers Limited," with the goal of establishing an environmental education center at the site. At their urging and with the support of Albany Mayor Erastus Corning, state officials visited the site to assess its appropriateness as an EEC.

The threatened closing of the Game Farm and Zoo made great press; it was a story that affected a very large number of people personally. The discussion in the newspapers helped prepare the public for the transition from a place with captive animals to a place dedicated to learning about nature. (Courtesy of the Times Union)

A planning group was formed, including local citizens and coordinated by DEC's Director of the Bureau of Education, Jerry E. Passer. It was probably this group that published a white paper, "Capital Area Environmental Education Center at Delmar (proposed)".

On November 19, 1971, Mr. Passer was able to report that

·Five Rivers Limited was completing its incorporation process, and the center would use "Five Rivers" in its name.

·Some staffing of the center would be undertaken by Passer and by Chuck McNulty and Wayne Trimm, also DEC staffers.

·A basic office was being set up, and plans were underway for an environmental library and an evening lecture series.

·Various regional and national organizations were being contacted for support.

Passer's report concluded on this note: "It's obvious that the plan is no longer a dream."

Though the NYS Department of Environmental Conservation was already contemplating an environmental education center for the Delmar site, the public outcry about the closing of the Game Farm undoubtedly helped to move the plan to the fast track. Even more importantly, it ensured funding for the start-up. (Courtesy of the Times Union)

How Did Five Rivers Get Its Name?

Visitors often ask, "Why is this place called 'Five Rivers'? I've only seen two streams!" The name reflects an understanding of our region as a great watershed, and underlines the purpose of Five Rivers Environmental Education Center: to teach the public about our environment, and to encourage them to be stewards of that environment.

In 1971, Vincent J. Schaefer, Director of SUNY Atmospheric Sciences Research Center, wrote a series of columns for the Knickerbocker News, then a daily newspaper of Albany. Calling his series "Five Rivers Rambles," Schaefer, a committed environmentalist, sought to awaken interest and concern in readers about the "beautiful land" of the greater Capital Region.

Focus

Five Rivers Rambles

What Have We Done to This Beautiful Land?

By
VINCENT
J.
SCHAEFER

Above: One of several articles from 1971-72 by Vincent Schae-
fer aimed at raising the public's environmental awareness.
(Courtesy of the Times Union)
Right: The five rivers for which the Center is named. (RA Fogarty)

This region, including all or parts of the Counties of Fulton, Saratoga, Washington, Montgom-
ery, Schenectady, Albany, Rensselaer, Schoharie, Green, and Columbia, is a watershed of five rivers:
the Schoharie Creek, the Mohawk River, the Sacandaga River, the Hoosic River, and the Hudson
River. These rivers all ultimately drain into the Hudson, creating a unique and integrated environment and history.

As an original board member of Friends of Five Rivers/Five Rivers Limited in 1972, Schaefer
suggested applying the Five Rivers name to the new environmental education center, as a reminder

that the Center would be more than simply a few hundred acres of protected habitat for public recreation. Located near the center of the Five Rivers region, it would become a center for learning about the larger environment, and a microcosm of the hills and streams, forests and farmland of east central New York.

Growth and Challenge

From the very beginning, funding was an issue for the Environmental Education Centers. The 1972 Environmental Quality Bond Act contained a budget of $1.2 billion, with $20 million earmarked for the development of environmental education centers. But the bond act's funding was cut by $50 million, including all funding for EECs. After lobbying by local senators, assemblymen, and citizens, two "member items" were added to the state budget: $100,000 for continuing support of Rogers, and $250,000 to begin development of Five Rivers.

The land on the northeast side of Heron and Beaver ponds was designated for the new center; the other side of the ponds would continue to be used by the Wildlife Research Center, still fully functioning. DEC's Chuck McNulty was appointed interim director to oversee preparations for the changed role of the Game Farm/Zoo site.

The Center Building had a checkered past, first as a temporary cafeteria at the State Office Campus, and then as the "Exhibit Shop" at the Game Farm. Un-insulated, with minimal ventilation, it is nonetheless focal point of environmental studies that continues to draw thousands of visitors each year. (Five Rivers Archives)

To prepare the site for use, an outdoor amphitheater and stage were built, and a network of hiking trails was begun. The exhibit shop (a temporary cafeteria building transported from the state office campus in the late 1960s) was refurbished to provide a visitors' center. Several Game Farm and CCC buildings were remodeled for use by environmental education and maintenance staff. Several CCC barracks buildings were demolished and the Game Farm's pens and fencing were removed.

The official opening was June 14, 1972. About a year later Robert Budliger became the Center's first fulltime director. Budliger worked with some seasonal employees to design programs. In April, 1974, environmental educators Alan Mapes and Patrician Delehanty joined him. The volunteers of Five Rivers Ltd. helped fill gaps in coverage and support.

The mission of the Center was to increase environmental awareness and provide educational services for children and adults. In 1976 the Center's significance was recognized when it became the state's first and only National Environmental Study Area. The federal designation has helped Five Rivers to survive through periods of budgetary uncertainty. As Holt Bodinson, Director of DEC's Division of Education in the 1970s, noted, "The value of a center lies in its permanence…It is very important that we have such places to turn to in our society."

Support from the Center's Many Constituents

Permanence and continuity have not been easy to achieve. The Center continued as a shoestring operation, with public demand for programs always exceeding staff capacity. In 1978 the Guided School Program (GSP), proposed by part-time staffer Grace Weatherby, came into existence to meet the demand for school classes. Drawn from volunteers and paid a nominal fee, the program's instructors were trained by DEC staff to teach an array of classes specific to the season. This program is described in more detail in Chapter 9.

The establishment of the Guided School Program was fortuitous. When the center's existence was threatened by budget cuts in 1980, the GSP instructors and the school teachers they served rallied public support to help prevent the closing. In April of 1980, with thousands of students already scheduled for GSP classes, the administration of then governor Hugh Carey announced the closing of Five Rivers due to state budget cuts. Alan Mapes, by 1980 the Center's director, and his other professional staffer, Wendy Repass Suozzo, received a letters from DEC Commissioner Robert

Flacke, announcing "with deep regret" their termination date of May 13.

Supporters of the Center went into action. The GSP instructors and the leadership of Five Rivers Ltd. contacted the media, gave interviews, circulated information to the public, and engineered a letter writing campaign from the teachers and children served by the GSP. Former Center Director Bob Budliger went outside of his own chain of command at DEC, calling Albany Mayor Erastus Corning. Corning, an early supporter, again came to the aid of the Center, talking with the Governor personally. The termination date was postponed until July, and then cancelled. The Center would remain open.

-4141   SCHENECTADY GAZETTE, WEDNESDAY, APRIL 30, 1980   GAZETTE PHONE 374-4141

Layoffs at Five Rivers Postponed to July 1—
Delmar Environmental Center Gets Stay for Spring

By STEVE NELSON
Gazette Reporter

ALBANY—Nearly 5,000 children were scheduled this spring to walk the leafy paths and trails of the state's environmental education center in Delmar before it was announced Monday the facility would be a victim of Governor Carey's budget cuts.

* * *

But those children may yet get their tour of the 270-acre Five Rivers Environmental Education Center on Game Farm Road. Alan Mapes, director of the seven-year-old facility, says he has received unofficial word the layoffs affecting the center will be rescinded until July 1.

Mapes, who is one of two full-time staff members scheduled to be laid off of May 13, says he spoke with superiors yesterday afternoon and learned the center would be allowed to operate through its spring season.

The center, on the site of the former Delmar Game Farm, was scheduled to be closed this Saturday as a result of the layoffs.

The farm is the only one of its kind in the Capital District and one of three in the entire state, says Mapes. The oldest one, which opened in 1967, is the Rogers Center in Sherbourne, a town outside Syracuse. The other center, the newest one, is in Beacon, across the Hudson River from Newburgh.

Between 35,000 and 40,000 persons took advantage of the center's program this year, according to Gerry Oakley, a member of Fiver Rivers Limited, a citizen support group for the center.

At least 20,000 of those visitors are school children, she says. Students from Saratoga, Schenectady, Rensselaer, Greene, Albany and Columbia counties have traveled to the facility for tours of the facility and its network of trails or for special environmental classes taught by members of the Five River Limited, says Oakley.

"Nothing else of this sort is available in this area," she claims.

"We are going to contact as many people as we can on this," says Oakley. "We are just starting to fight." Her organization has between 25 and 35 persons at any one time to act as instructors for various tours and programs offered at the center.

One of the most popular programs offered is the star walk. The walk is offered to the public often, says Mapes, and has been enhanced by the presence of a local astronomy club, which supplies telescopes to provide a close-up look at celestial bodies.

The various nature walks are high on the popularity list as well, he says.

"We have probably 100 species or more of wild flowers on the site. About 165 different species of birds have visited the center over the past five years," says Mapes. Over 60 different species has been sighted this year, he claims.

"It is not a tremendous ecological gem of a place," he says. "But it offers a good variety of habitats."

—(Gazette Photo—Ed Schultz) er is all the Capital District has. rild flowers and more than 165 says it costs about $50,000 per

Five Rivers continued to be vulnerable to funding shortfalls, having no line item of its own in the state budget. (Courtesy of the Daily Gazette)

The Original Fall Festival

On September 13, 1980, the Center held an open house, announcing that

Because of the support given by you
and many others
we would like to take this opportunity
to THANK YOU and to
INVITE YOU AND YOUR FAMILY
To
FIVE RIVERS ENVIRONMENTAL EDUCATION CENTER'S
OPEN HOUSE

The open house featured trail walks, demonstrations, activities, and refreshments. This was the inception of the annual Five Rivers Fall Festival, which continues today as a celebration of the successful partnership of volunteers and professional staff that kept the Center open.

Attention to Archaeology and History on Site

Recognition of the site's historical significance has been an ongoing feature of Five Rivers. In 1983 when a U.S. postage stamp commemorating the Civilian Conservation Corps was issued, a ceremony marking the event was held at the Center. In 1992 when a municipal water line was planned through the Center lands, the state commissioned an archaeological and historical study, employing Collamer and Associates, Inc., to assess the historic interest of the site and to identify archaeological resources. The study provided valuable insights for this history.

After reviewing the historical development of the area and carrying out "intensive visual reconnaissance of the project area and the excavation of shovel test units," the researchers concluded as follows:

Since the Five Rivers Environmental Education Center is situated in a region considered to be highly sensitive for the location of both prehistoric and early historic cultural resources, a cultural resource management plan for the park should be considered. This plan could outline sections of the park which have high, moderate, or low probability for the location of archaeological data. Construction in the highly sensitive regions could thereby be avoided, thus preserving these non-renewable resources. In addition to protecting cultural resources, the management plan would provide valuable information for future use and planning. (p. 31.)

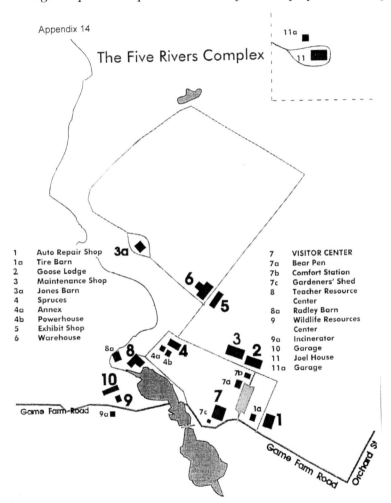

Appendix 14

The Five Rivers Complex

1	Auto Repair Shop		7	VISITOR CENTER
1a	Tire Barn		7a	Bear Pen
2	Goose Lodge		7b	Comfort Station
3	Maintenance Shop		7c	Gardeners' Shed
3a	Jones Barn		8	Teacher Resource Center
4	Spruces			
4a	Annex		8a	Radley Barn
4b	Powerhouse		9	Wildlife Resources Center
5	Exhibit Shop			
6	Warehouse		9a	Incinerator
			10	Garage
			11	Joel House
			11a	Garage

In 1993, Center staff and volunteers mounted an exhibit portraying the recent history of the site in time for the Bethlehem Bicentennial celebration in 1993. Eagle Scout Troop 73 even produced a Five Rivers Historical Bicentennial Bike Route. Later, Craig Thompson, Center director from 1995 to the present and himself a history buff, produced materials for a "Self-Guided Historical Tour" of the Center. Thompson has also been responsible for an article in *The Conservationist* about the CCC, and an exhibit on the subject at the New Scotland Historical Association.

Because of its historic background, Five Rivers never presents itself as a "wilderness" environment. Instead, the Center tries to maintain a variety of habitats: woodland, orchard, meadow, pond, and wetland—in order to maximize the environmental education potential of the site. (Five Rivers Environmental Education Center Draft Unit Management Plan, February 2007)

Still another archaeological dig took place in 2001-2 as a result of another proposed water line. This investigation was not within Five Rivers boundaries, but nearby, on property owned by James Tate, a past president of the Friends of Five Rivers. The Hartgen Archaeological team made a number of interesting discoveries, that suggest what type of forest existed in the area, and how precontact people used it. The team concluded in its report that:

> *The tight grouping of sites found with Five Rivers including the Tate Site supports the interpretation that the Five Rivers region was a focal point for precontact occupation. With the new supportive data provided by the Phase III excavations and recent research combined in this report we have begun to interpret the relationship and how the relationship occurs between the sites at Five Rivers. The Five Rivers region as a whole is important to understanding a part of precontact settlement in the mid-Hudson Valley that was of significance during the cold half of the year. (p. 26.)*

This "deep history" aspect of Five Rivers affirms yet again the importance of open, undeveloped space in the most heavily settled regions.

A Rich and Diverse Program

Through a process that today would be called "continuous quality improvement," Five Rivers Center expanded and consolidated its programs during the 1980s and 1990s. The annual Fall Festival was just one such offering to the public. The Guided School Program continued to flourish, serving growing numbers of elementary school classes every year. For over thirty years, the program has been presenting classes to between 4,000 and 6,000 students per year.

Volunteers were trained to assist the DEC staff: assistant naturalists and junior naturalists, who helped present evening and weekend programs to the public, and volunteers helped with bird counts, bat observations, studies of monarch butterflies and fireflies, and other ongoing research.

By the 1990s, the Center was presenting eighty to a hundred weekend and evening programs a year, keyed to the natural phenomena that could be observed on site. Fall brought topics like "All about Bats," "Forest Pests," and "Are There Bears Here?" In winter snowshoes came out, and programs covered such topics as animal tracks, owls, and maple sugaring. Spring would bring programs on the arrival of bluebirds and other migratory birds, and the emergence of turtles, spring wildflowers, and stream and pond organisms.

Above left: Kitty Rusch, who began as an intern and was hired as an environmental educator at Five Rivers, takes advantage of a "teachable moment" with visitors. (Five Rivers Archives)

Above right: Craig Thompson has served as Director of Five Rivers since 1995. He has been an articulate advocate for both the natural and the historical dimensions of Five Rivers. (Photo by RA Fogarty)

Right: With the Goose Lodge as a base, the Guided School Program has taken four to six thousand students per year on outdoor adventures and learning experiences. (Photo by RA Fogarty)

In summer the Center sponsored day camps for families, featuring orienteering, insects and stream life, animal signs, and sketching from nature. The week-long, half-day programs were unique in engaging parents with their children in outdoor activity.

In addition, the center began to offer programs featuring alternative energy and recycling: "Go Green at Home," "Eco-Friendly Wrapping," and "America Recycles." The annual spring Earth Day becomes Earth Week at the Center, with a number of events and programs.

The Center staff have been leaders in the environmental training of teachers. Project WILD (wildlife-focused conservation education), Project WET (worldwide water education), and PLT (Project Learning Tree) have been used to involve school teachers in hands-on environmental science. Staff and interns also take programs to the schools, most recently, the "Nature's Schoolyard" program. "Tails by Mail," another resource for teachers, provides 2-week loan-out boxes of nature specimens, books, posters, and teaching ideas for hands-on use in classrooms. The Center also offers three-week summer teacher fellowships. Environmental interns trained at the center help with teaching classes, work on collection maintenance, and assist staff in creating educational displays for the Center.

Both the trail guides (above) and trailhead signage (facing page) have improved over the years. The emphasis is on providing outdoor experiences in a variety of habitats, such as woodland, stream, pond, and meadow. (Photo by RA Fogarty)

Trails

The network of trails at the Center was created early, but has been repeatedly rehabilitated and enhanced. It now measures a total of approximately eight miles. Over time the Center staff developed trail guides and print materials on a variety of nature subjects, for visitors to use on self-guided walks on the trails.

In 1978, a Youth Conservation Corps group led by DEC staffer Jim Suozzo developed the Woodlot Trail. This would then be upgraded in the early 1980's to make it handicapped accessible, using planks to deck wet areas and compacted stone dust on the rest.

In addition to the Woodlot Trail, the Center received the gift of a paved handicapped accessible trail in 1997 from Five Rivers Ltd. (by this time using the name Friends of Five Rivers). "Nature's Backyard Trail" is described in more detail in Chapter 9.

One item that has been a continual "work in progress" is a comprehensive trail map for the center. At one point in the early 2000s, a small duplicated map of the trails was replaced by an attractive glossy printed map, but the supply was soon exhausted and there were no funds to continue printing it. Now, thanks to website improvements, an excellent map of the Center is available on the DEC website at: http://www.dec.ny.gov/docs/administration_pdf/5rivermap.pdf

The Center Building: Lemons to Lemonade

The Center building itself (still that prefabricated cafeteria moved to the Center in the 1960s), is a funky and fascinating place, especially for children. In the lobby, nature artist Wayne Trimm's mural wall is broken up by windows into aquariums that house native fish and turtle species. A large cage houses the current barred owl, Aries, one of a series of injured owls who have made the Center their home.

Wayne Trimm has illustrated many New York State publications over the years. As shown here, his talents were applied early in the life of Five Rivers to helping turn a recycled building into a genuine environmental education center. His mural in the entrance area of the Center Building features the diversity of life in and around a wetland. Aquariums built into the wall hold small turtles, snakes, and fish. (Five Rivers Archives)

There is a revolving series of wall displays on topics from "Name that Scat" to "Wildflower Identification." Frequently a show of art, photos, or artifacts will be on display. Children gather at a large display table with "found objects" for them to handle: animal skulls, beaver-chewed wood, pinecones, nuts, and bones.

In the "Classroom" beyond the lobby, the current bird list (including the name of each birder who spotted a species first!) hangs in one corner. A large window opens on a view of the bird feeding area. Benches, a couch, bird books, and a speaker transmitting bird sounds from outside make this one of the most popular places in the Center. One corner features a working beehive. The walls are lined with taxidermy of native species, and a framed case of birds' wings. A "Five Rivers Hall of Fame" graces one side of the room. (See the Appendix).

The touch table is a favorite with preschoolers, who love examining the skulls, bones, fur pelts, pinecones, and other objects from nature. It reflects the "hands-on science" philosophy that emerged in education in the 1970s and 80s. (Photo by RA Fogarty)

Both old and young, the mobile and the handicapped can enjoy the bird viewing area in the Center. Equipped with binoculars and bird identification manuals, it gives hours of viewing pleasure, especially in winter. In compliance with recent policies, the Center does not feed birds except in winter, to avoid problems with nuisance wildlife. (Photo by RA Fogarty)

This shoestring facility has its limitations: poor ventilation, little insulation, antiquated restrooms, and endemic overcrowding. Still, the Center building is regarded with affection by the volunteers, staff, and the public, for whom it represents the warm center of a wonderful outdoor world.

The Centers collection of taxidermied mammals and birds allows visitors to appreciate species that they will probably never see close-up in the wild. (Photo by RA Fogarty)

The multipurpose classroom in the Center is in constant use for classes, meetings, and events. The "Hall of Fame" on the front wall, started by Craig Thompson, memorializes many of the people discussed in these pages. It is reproduced in Appendix A of this book. (Photo by RA Fogarty)

Land Acquisition

A definitive map of Five Rivers has been a moving target, partly because the Center has grown from its initial 120 acres in 1933 to 446 acres as of 2011. Land acquisitions came in the form of gifts, and of purchases by the state, some facilitated by Five Rivers Ltd. (now known as Friends of Five Rivers) and /or the Open Space Institute (OSI), a not-for-profit which channels grant funds to the preservation of open space. The table below chronicles the land acquisitions that have occurred over the lifetime of New York State's involvement with the site.

PARCEL	GRANTOR	PURCHASER	ACREAGE	DATE
1	Edward Ackerman	NYCD	1.0	3/1933
2	Edward Ackerman	NYCD	112.3	3/1933
3	Ira Smith	NYCD	4.5	3/1933
4	Ernest Miller	NYCD	2.9	7/1933
5	Ariel Morehouse	NYCD	.7	7/1934
6	John Martt	NYCD	2.6	8/1934
7	John Martt	NYCD	13.0	11/1937
8	Edward Ackerman	NYCD	94.0	1/1939
9	Richard Herrman	NYSDEC	14.4	1973
10	Donald Hoenig	NYSDEC	2.4	1973
11	Albany County	NYSDEC	.2	1979
12	Avis Morehouse	NYSDEC	81.8	1989
13	Frances Bishop	FFR / NYSDEC	17.5	1996
14	Carol Foresman	GIFT	6.0	2001
15	Robert Joel	NYSDEC	50.0	2001
16	OSI/Donald Miller	OSI / NYSDEC	43.0	2006
			TOTAL: 446.3	

Data are from Five Rivers Environmental Education Center Draft Unit Management Plan, February 2007

Five Rivers Land Acquisitions

First Parcel
February 25, 1933
1 acre

March 1933
113 acres

1934
124 acres

1937
137 acres

1939
230 acres

1974
247 acres

1979
261 acres

1989
328 acres

1996
346 acres

2001
400 acres

2006
445 acres

The black outline shows the current size of the Five Rivers property. The dark shading indicates the size of property in the year indicated. All acreage figures have been rounded up.

To Plan or Not to Plan, To Build or Not to Build

At any site of natural or historical interest, any hint of change becomes fraught with thorny questions. As a site having both natural *and* historical interest, Five Rivers has had its share of controversy. Add to this the strong emotional ties between the Five Rivers Center and the surrounding communities, and one can see the potential for strong feelings pro and con any proposed change.

Many printed plans for the Center's future have been created. Bob Budliger reported that the Rogers Center staff visited Delmar in 1971 and wrote a suggested program outline for the new Center. National Audubon Society's Nature Center Planning Division staff met with him in 1974 and wrote recommendations, and he himself wrote a Center plan in 1978. In 1987, Friends of Five Rivers/Five Rivers Ltd. produced a Master Plan for the Center at the urging of then DEC Commissioner Henry Williams. This was updated each year through 1990. The Friends group then, in 1993, redesigned the planning document to serve as a resource tool. The new plan provided

The Center has grown from its original acreage to 446 acres. (Five Rivers Environmental Education Center Draft Unit Management Plan, February 2007)

- A list of the 1987 recommendations;
- A 1993 status report on each of those recommendations;
- A four-page section on "ongoing concerns";
- A brief history and site description;
- A detailed program description with recommendations;
- A series of maps;
- Checklists of birds and wildflowers observed at the Center.

The report contains an attached letter signed by Friends president Dave Rhodes and Center Director Al Mapes agreeing that solvents and other hazardous chemicals used at the site would be contained and disposed of off-site. Clearly vigilant staff and volunteers had raised the issue.

In 2005 DEC commissioned the NYS Office of General Services to do a study preliminary to providing a master plan for the so-called "intensive use area" of Five Rivers. The impetus was an offer of $500,000 by an anonymous donor to provide a new building for the Guided School Program. OGS unfortunately produced its report with little or no input from staff and volunteers. The result was a plan that was unacceptable to both the donor and the people working at Five Rivers.

In 2007, a long-awaited *Unit Management Plan* was issued for public comment. The plan, required under DEC regulations for each of its sites, was explained at a series of somewhat hastily scheduled public meetings in winter and early spring of 2007. Two features of the plan raised controversy and overshadowed the many strong features of the document.

First of all, a *Schematic Design Narrative* and floor plan for a new center building, prepared by Lewis Engineering P.C. for the Office of General Services, was attached to the report. This proved to be a red flag to staff and volunteers, who saw again a nearly completed design on which they had had no input. The plan also projected demolition of several of the centers older buildings, some of which had historical significance.

Second, the plan contained language that seemed to leave the door open to hunting and trapping at Five Rivers. Alarmed locals envisioned months of the year when Five Rivers trails would be off-limits or unsafe for use by the public as a result of this heretofore-unheard-of use of the Center lands. Citizens attending the public meetings, including hunters, were outspokenly opposed to the idea.

Friends of Five Rivers issued a twenty-three-page response to the plan, which then seemed

Goose Lodge, though the home of the Guided School Program for many years, had definite drawbacks, lack of space being one. Sometimes as many as six or eight instructors had to pack their equipment at the same time. (Five Rivers Archives)

to disappear from view, although a revision of the plan was apparently completed in late 2007, according to DEC central office staff. Completion was never formally announced in DEC's Environmental Notice Bulletin; however, a version of the plan is available online.

Efforts at planning have been hampered over the years: first, by failure to consult all affected parties; second, by lack of funds for proposals and; third, by frequent changes in administration (and therefore of program priorities) at the state and department levels.

Recently, by dint of strenuous communication efforts, work on a new Guided School Program building was finally begun, taking advantage of the original half-million dollar gift offered in 2005. Although DEC continued to have concerns about the project, a Bethlehem Town Board member, Sam Messina, made contact with the Governor's Deputy Secretary for Energy and the Environment, Judith Enck. Through their good offices, an agreement was brokered that was acceptable to all. The half-million dollar gift would be used to purchase all the materials for the project. DEC would pay for the architectural plans, and DEC Operations would provide equipment and construction personnel. Special funding would pay for installation of an energy efficient geothermal heating system.

If the state funding ever becomes available, this architectural plan will extend to a new Center building across a courtyard from the GSP building. The two buildings in combination will qualify as Energy Star compliant.

The new GSP Program building, a co-operative project of the Repass family, the Friends of Five Rivers, and NYS-DEC, will house the school program in more adequate facilities and meet other needs as well. The building is part of a comprehensive architectural plan by Envision Architects, that includes a new Center building near the GSP building. Completing the plan would produce a LEAD certified facility, but state budget limits may push the realization of the full plan well into the future. (Photo by RA Fogarty)

The Indispensable Government/Community Partnership

In every case, finances have been an overriding factor in planning for Five Rivers. Not only are funds in perennial short supply; the annual state budget cycle creates constant uncertainty about which staff and programs will continue from year to year. In this situation, state facilities and their staffs can become helpless pawns in a never-ending struggle for resources. As the 40th anniversary of Five Rivers is celebrated in 2012, the DEC center staff has shrunk to three,

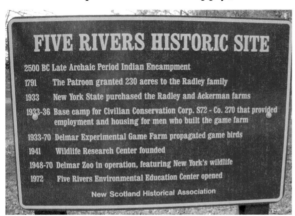

Recently New Scotland Historical Association arranged for the placement of this historical marker at the center. Though the Center is frequently identified with Delmar and Bethlehem, the majority of the land is within the Town of New Scotland. (Photo by RA Fogarty)

Things come full circle at the Five Rivers 40th Anniversary celebration on June 16, 2012. Current DEC Commissioner Joe Martens chats with Lois Gundrum, president of the Audubon Society of the Capital Region. In her remarks to the assembled group, Gundrum pointed out that the Society had helped to start Five Rivers, which in turn has helped with support and facilities to keep the Society going. (Photo by RA Fogarty)

taking the center back to late 1970s levels. (Two of DEC's four environmental education centers have lost all staff.) Maintenance services are at an all-time low, and the Center building is no longer open on Sundays.

Even more fundamental than finances, however, has been the human factor. The Center has had the good fortune to attract staff and volunteers of exceptional caliber. Many Center staff have emerged as leaders in their respective specialties. The Appendix catalogs a "Hall of Fame" of many of these individuals, a display also mounted in the Center building.

As noted at the beginning of this chapter, the commitment and love of ordinary citizens for Five Rivers has been fundamental to its survival. We turn next to the story of that citizen commitment.

Chapter 8 Resources

Budliger, Robert. Review of *"Five Rivers History"*. January, 2012

Capital Area Environmental Education Center at Delmar (proposed). (Undated proposal and proposed map, from the files of Five Rivers Limited.)

Collamer and Associates, Inc. *Stage 1A and Stage 1B Cultural Resource Investigations for Five Rivers Environmental Education Center, Wildlife Resources Center, Delmar Waterline Project.* (114 Gardner Hill, East Nassau, NY 12062) September 30, 1992

Five Rivers Limited. *Five Rivers Environmental Education Center Master Plan: Prepared for the Department of Environmental Conservation by the Directors of Five Rivers Limited, Inc., in Consultation with the Staff of Five Rivers Center.* March 1, 1987 (From the files of Five Rivers Limited.)

Five Rivers Limited. *Five Rivers Master Plan: 1993 Update.* (From the files of Five Rivers Limited.)

Five Rivers Limited. *Board Minutes: 1972-1993.* (From the files of Five Rivers Limited.)

Hartgen Archaeological Associates, Inc. *The Tate Site: Phase III Data Retrieval Investigation.* (1744 Washington Ave. Extension, Rensselaer, NY 12144) March, 2002.

Mapes, Alan. Comments on *"Five Rivers History"*. February 22, 2012.

NYS Department of Environmental Conservation. *Five Rivers Environmental Education Center: Draft Unit Management Plan: Albany Country, Towns of New Scotland and Bethlehem.* February 2007.

NYS Office of General Services. *Program Report: Study to provide a Master Plan: Five Rivers Environmental Education Center, 56 Game Farm Road, Project No. S1469.* July 1, 2005.

Oakley, Gerry. Comments on *"Five Rivers History."* January 25, 2012

Passer, Jerry. *Assorted memoranda.* In *Board Minutes: 1972-1993.* (From the files of Five Rivers Limited.)

Payne, Nancy. Comments on *"Five Rivers History."* February, 2012

25th Birthday Celebration, June 14, 1997. (Invitational flyer from the files of Five Rivers Limited.)

Weatherby, Grace E. Comments on *"Five Rivers History."* January 28, 2012.

Weatherby, Grace E. History of Five Rivers Limited Guided Program (Memorandum, 1988.)

Above: Instructor with a Guided School Program group. (Friends of Five Rivers Archives)

Left: Volunteer Gerry Langhauser constructing a storage shed. (Photo by RA Fogarty)

Below: Greeter Connie Tilroe covering the front desk on a Saturday morning. (Photo by RA Fogarty)

CHAPTER 9

"THE FRIENDS"

FRIENDS OF FIVE RIVERS/FIVE RIVERS LIMITED

"There lies before me the most beautiful land the eyes of man ever beheld."
Arendt Van Curler, 1643

In my opinion, the time is at hand when all of us must join hands
and consider the welfare of the land and all who live here....
Love of beauty, natural and otherwise, is not limited to just a few....
If successful, we will no longer need to be concerned about
the future quality of land and water in "the beautiful land."

Vincent J. Schaefer
Five Rivers Rambles: What Have We Done to This Beautiful Land:
The Knickerbocker News/Union Star, April 15, 1971

Friends of Five Rivers, a private, not-for-profit association of volunteers originally incorporated as Five Rivers Ltd., is so intertwined with Five Rivers Environmental Education Center that many people think they are one and the same. This mistake is a tribute to the almost seamless cooperative relationship that exists between all the partners at the Center: the DEC Center director, the staff of environmental educators, Friends of Five Rivers' Board of Directors, seasonal interns, Friends' paid staff, and volunteers.

Such a relationship could never have been planned; it had to evolve. In Chapter 8 we discussed the establishment of the Center at the urging of private citizens and public officials. Over the forty years of Five Rivers' existence, the state's commitment has fluctuated and wavered: DEC staffing has ranged from one to seven at different times; the center was threatened with closure more than once. "The Friends" and its volunteers, therefore, have been the constant, stepping up when needed with funding and personnel.

Launching "Five Rivers Limited"

In early 1972, interested citizens drew up articles of incorporation for "Five Rivers Limited," stating that "The purposes for which the corporation is to be formed are:

To engage in, foster, and promote the study of, education in and appreciation for natural resources, natural sciences and all ecological matters, as well as all aspects of man-made environment and their relationship with people; to engage in surveys and other research and instruction of all kinds, to initiate programs and to make available and accessible to the public the resources controlled by the corporation, including but not limited to collection and land and buildings owned or controlled by the corporation, including, but by no means limited to, facilities in the Town of New Scotland; to encourage the participation of the general public in the activities of the corporation. (Bylaws of Five Rivers Limited, p. 1.)

The language of the statement of purpose reflects the possibility, briefly considered, that the corporation itself might take over the old Game Farm site. The application for incorporation was signed by John P. MacArthur, Eric Leighton, Sandy Shoor, Saul Caro, and Robert Nurnberger. Incorporation of "Five Rivers Limited" was granted on February 3, 1972.

Then there was apparently a hiatus. Perhaps each of the parties, the state agency and the citizens' group, was waiting for the other to pick up the ball. In a memorandum to Saul Caro dated August 8, 1972, DEC Education Bureau Chief Jerry Passer says

"There is a critical need for the first annual meeting of the Five Rivers Corporation....[There is a need to] actually implement some of the ideas and suggestions that have resulted from considerable citizen involvement and participation to date."

It is unclear from Passer's memo who was responsible for the inertia that followed the state's commitment to establish the center and the citizens' incorporation as a not-for-profit. However, Passer refers to "much unfavorable criticism" and a "considerable credibility gap." One senses that the fledging effort to establish an environmental education center at Five Rivers is at a crisis point.

Early Center director Bob Budliger provided his perspective for this period, saying that both Five

Capitol Area Environmental Education Center at Delmar
(proposed)

What is an environmental education center?

As demonstrated by the Rogers Conservation Education Center at Sherburne, N. Y., such a spot provides, in an outdoor setting, a variety of learning experiences, all of which relate to man's place in the ecology of the world in which he lives. Through the use of visual aids, laboratories, observation stations, demonstration areas, labeled interpretive trails, wildlife exhibits, and special study areas, the knowledge of man's own relationship to the natural world is made available, fascinating and exciting. Designed for use by all ages, from the very young to the senior citizen, the Environmental Education Center provides the story of ecology, presented in a simple and clear manner.

Programs prepared for school groups are designed to coordinate with school curricula. They provide field experiences and instruction by specialists in environmental quality and resource management not normally available at most schools. The level of instruction is adaptable to all grade levels, from elementary to college. In addition, programs for individual visitors and family groups are regularly presented. Facilities of the Center are sometimes used for cooperative research projects with personnel from nearby schools and colleges.

The variety of landscapes surrounding the Center, including woodlands, fields, and old orchards. A well-developed road network was built in the early thirties by men of a CCC camp which then occupied the site. Stones from the old Erie Canal were used to rip-rap roadside banks. Many of the buildings were also built by CCC men. Some of these buildings have been eliminated over the years, but others have been used since 1940 to house wildlife exhibits. There is also an exhibits fabrication shop, and an area of the property is used for the Wildlife Research Laboratory and Pathology Unit of the Department of Environmental Conservation.

With the phasing out of the game propagation program at Delmar much of the land and some of the buildings have become available for other uses. We feel that the Delmar Game Farm site can be adapted for use as an environmental education center.

Its use as an education and information center is further enhanced by its proximity to the Capital District and large urban, suburban and rural populations. Year-round accessibility and diversity of physical features and the availability of existing structures further support its development in the manner suggested.

What must be done to have this site become the Capital Area Environmental Education Center?

site, a tremendous potential for developing an environmental education center which could be outstanding in our state, and probably in our country. The specialists of the Division of Educational Services of the New York State Department of Environmental Conservation have the knowledge to implement such a plan. The land is available. What is needed now is public interest and help.

What kind of help is needed to make a Capital District Environmental Education Center become a reality at Delmar?

It is important that community organizations, citizens, and the educational community understand this proposal in concept. Their endorsement of it will be most influential in securing the funding and manpower needs necessary for the development and programming of the Center. Ultimately, the Center will be most successful and properly serve the users for which it is intended if its plan is cooperatively executed. Public assistance and support will therefore be requested on many fronts.

Many have expressed a feeling of frustration in dealing with environmental problems, and have wished for a tangible means of becoming involved. Here is an opportunity to participate in a project which could be of benefit locally and might have far-reaching results. For it is only through understanding of man's relationship to the living and non-living

The earliest public document on Five Rivers poses five questions: What is an environmental education center?-- Could the Delmar Game Farm site be adapted for use as a center?— What must be done to have this site become a center?—What kind of help is needed?—How shall I express my interest? It concludes: What is needed now is public interest and help....A Capital District Environmental Education Center can become a meeting place for learning and for enjoying the full promise of... the environment of the future. (Five Rivers Archives)

The proposal had this diagram on the reverse side. The white paper was unsigned and was not attributed to any organization, so it is unclear whether it was a DEC product, came from the Five Rivers Ltd. group., or was a product of the joint meetings chaired by Jerry Passer. (Five Rivers Archives)

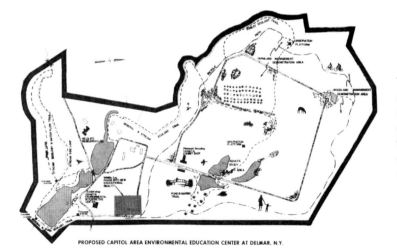

PROPOSED CAPITOL AREA ENVIRONMENTAL EDUCATION CENTER AT DELMAR, N.Y.

Rivers Limited and DEC were struggling. The Five Rivers Limited group had disagreements over whether the Center should be directed by them, as a tax-exempt not-for-profit, or by DEC. Meanwhile, various units at DEC were in a struggle among themselves for control of this unique site. At the same time, there was no assurance of state funding for a center, and no Civil Service plan for staffing it.

The earliest newsletters from the Center were dated May, July, August, and September, 1972. Produced by Edythe Caro, Janice Hornbach, Sigrin Newell, and Jerry Passer, they make fascinating reading. One article describes the first use of the Center amphitheater: a benefit concert for victims of Hurricane Agnes. Lena Spencer of Café Lena presided, with several well-known artists and groups performing. (Five Rivers Archives)

On September 30, 1972, a meeting was held to elect a board of directors for the Five Rivers Limited corporation. A handwritten sign-up sheet lists the members of the first board of directors: Eric Leighton, Robert Nurnburger, Sandy Shoor, Stanton Baltzel, Bernice Leighton, Sigrin Newell, and Vincent J. Schaefer. Albany mayor Erastus Corning had been an advocate for the center from the beginning, and would later serve on the board himself. He may have encouraged Vincent Schaefer, Director of Atmospheric Sciences Research Center, to lend his name and credibility to the first board of directors.

The notes also show that at this point the corporation had a balance of $1050 in the bank. The next few months must have witnessed the challenge of busy people trying to launch an all-volunteer organization, with no staff, no budget, and little time.

The first written minutes, dated November 7, 1972, reflect what would become perennial issues:
- DEC/Friends communication;
- facilities for the educational program;
- the group's role in equipping the Center and it's programs (chairs, snowshoes, and trail bridges were among the expenses being discussed);
- building the Friends' membership;
- structuring the Friends' work (committees on membership, public relations, program, and administration were established).

The group met again on December 6, 1972. By this time, more basic issues had emerged:

- need for a memo of understanding between DEC and "the corporation" (i.e. Five Rivers Limited);
- applying for tax exempt status;
- importance of a membership drive;
- need for a long term master plan for the Center.

At a January 3, 1973 meeting, committees were added for facilities, fiscal matters, and public action, as well as an executive committee of the Board. Attorney John P. MacArthur was drafting bylaws for the group, which was also discussing bigger issues:

- urging the state legislature to set aside funds for environmental education;
- applying for grants for curriculum development and community education;
- acquiring land to expand the Center.

The Board called a general meeting of the membership for April 28, 1973. The agenda mentions a review of the steps already taken to establish the Center, the introduction of just-arrived Center Director Bob Budliger, cooperative plans for upcoming Center programs (a summer course for children, monthly public programs in fall, trail walks, movies), and uses for membership dues.

By the May 9, 1973, Board meeting, the group was discussing permanent committees, publishing trail guides, and liability coverage for volunteers. Soon an annual meeting for the corporation was scheduled for November 1, 1973. Bylaws were adopted. One has the sense that the organization has turned the corner, that the precarious early effort has become permanent.

Five Rivers Limited: An Evolving Entity

In early fall of 1973, the first issue of a Five Rivers Limited newsletter, titled "Quarterly Notes," was mailed out. Then president Robert Nurnberger announced the upcoming first annual meeting of the corporation and gave a progress report:

Placing the positive first, during the first year of operation, 15,000 students and teachers participated in programs at the Center. A great number of individuals came to walk our trails and ask question. Forty-two children of corporation members took part in special summer programs. In addition such organizations as the Cub Scouts, Helderberg Workshop, and the International Center used the facility during the summer months. The initial Beaver Tree Trail has been improved and two other trails have been developed. Cooperative programs with BOCES initiated by the Board have now passed the planning stage. Local teachers have been able to participate in environmental training courses for university credit. There have been frequent orientation workshops for teachers. Summer movie and lecture programs for the general public were very successful. (p. 1.)

This aerial photo shows the controversial maintenance shop and tire barn, in the large paved area at the right. (Five Rivers Archives)

Nurnberger went on, however, to complain about "conflicting uses" of the site. The presence of the DEC automotive maintenance shop and warehouse were a sore spot that would continue to chafe for years. The other issue raised was that "our concerns and aspirations relative to the development of the Center" be heard. Perhaps with the arrival of paid DEC staff, the volunteers were feeling insecure about their role and voice in the Center's future.

Five Rivers Limited (FRL) volunteers were soon covering the front desk as needed, sending out the newsletter to the membership, making small purchases to support the Center, and advocating with DEC and the legislature for expansion of the educational programs at the Center. In 1975 FRL and DEC signed a memo of understanding, acknowledging and defining the supportive and advisory role of the Friends. The agreement, revised in 1982, states DEC's primary role in providing and implementing public information and education programs, and encourages Friends support and participation.

In Chapter 8 the threatened closing of the Center in 1980 was discussed, and the response by volunteers. This response was largely orchestrated by the Friends Board and volunteer Geraldine "Gerry" Oakley. In 1981 Gerry became FRL's first paid administrator, also taking over coordination of the Guided School Program. With its own staff member (albeit for only fifteen hours a week), the Friends group was able to accomplish more, in a more organized fashion. Gerry proved to be a vital asset, continuing her involvement for over thirty years, long past her official retirement as administrator in 1993.

Gerry was followed in the administrator's position by Leda Loux, who worked for the Friends for 18 years and facilitated a period of growth in programs and services. On Leda's retirement in 2011 she was replaced by Joann Macklin, current FFR administrator and an experienced not-for-profit manager.

Under the changing leadership of the Friends' Board, the activities of the organization expanded to meet new challenges. The fact that the bylaws limit Board members to a maximum of three three-year terms means that there are new members introducing new ideas on a regular basis. The Board has been led over the years by a succession of committed presidents, each one serving for one or at most two two-year terms:

1972-4	Robert Nurnberger	1990-92	John Meany
1974-6	C. Stanton Baltzel	1992-94	David Rhodes
1976-7	William Matott	1994-8	James Tate
1977-82	Catherine Van Volkenburgh	1998-2002	Marge Farrell
1982-86	Margaret Hay	2002-06	Dan Lewis
1986-88	Robert Alexander	2006-10	RoseAnne Fogarty
1988-90	Karol Harlow	2010-present	Richard Bader

A few highlights of the Friends' evolving mission include the following:
- **Paying for or facilitating land acquisition:**
  - 1996: Friends acquire 17.5 acres from Frances Bishop through a fundraising effort, re-selling the property to DEC;
  - 1999: Early board member Carol Foresman donates six acres of family property to Friends of Five Rivers, which signs it over to DEC in 2001;
  - 2006: The Open Space Institute acquires the 43-acre Miller parcel for DEC, with assistance from the Friends.
- **Acting as an advocate for environmental education**
  - 1980: Friends contact legislators to prevent Center closing;
  - 1994: Friends successfully oppose staff cuts;
  - 2011: Friends urge DEC to maintain staff at Five Rivers during state budget crisis.

° **Providing funds for program needs as they arose:**

   ° 1977: A router for making trail signs;

   ° 1980s: Books for the library, the Center's first computer; a bee hive for the orchard, and mice for Archimedes, the barred owl;

   ° 1990s to present: Grant money to support several environmental interns each year, (with partial reimbursement from DEC, depending on available funds);

   ° 2009: Repairs to the water control system at the Center; new floating dock near Goose Pond;

   ° 2000-2011: An electronic golf cart, a rechargeable weed whacker, and handicapped accessible binoculars for the handicapped accessible trail; a display beehive and taxidermy specimens for the Center classroom;

   ° 2012 (under current consideration): remote cameras for wildlife observation and population assessment; digital signage.

Important ongoing activities for Friends of Five Rivers include land protection, fund raising through selling bird seed, and organizing the Fall Festival (Five Rivers Archives)

Many of the Friends' purchases of equipment and supplies for the Center have been made possible by gifts from living members, as well as memorial gifts by the family and friends of deceased people who had a special love for Five Rivers, of whom there have been many. The generosity of these donors, too numerous to name, has made the Friends a conduit for the community's good will toward the Center and its programs.

The Guided School Program: A Lighthouse in Environmental Education

In 1975, volunteer and part-time staffer Grace Weatherby made a proposal that would lead to a surge in the Center's use and popularity. She pointed out that the DEC staffers were already unable to meet the burgeoning demand for school classes. If the staff provided lesson plans and training for volunteers, the impact of the Center's school program could be increased exponentially. After lengthy discussion the staff agreed, and training started in September 1978. A few volunteers were trained in and taught a few autumn classes in "Animal Signs" and "Exploring Nature."

An initial report to the Board on January 24, 1979, showed that over twenty instructors had been trained in December 1978 and January 1979 in "Wildlife in Winter" and "Snowshoeing and Winter Ecology." Four classes with a total of 102 students had already been taught; nine classes were scheduled, for another 281 students. Work had begun on spring lessons: "Spring Explorations;" "Stream Life;" "Animal Signs;" "World of the Pond," and "Forest Life."

Here participating in GSP training are (l. to r.) Mary Lou Riccardo, Noreen Van Cans, Robin Smith, Judy Gross Johnson, Jackie Citriniti, and Wendy Suozzo. (Friends of Five Rivers Archives)

Lesson plans were written by Wendy Repass Suozzo, assisted by Grace Weatherby and with support from then Center Director Al Mapes. Grace Weatherby was the first GSP coordinator, with a small salary from Five Rivers Ltd. With Wendy Suozzo, she examined trails for appropriate teaching sites, and bought the needed supplies, equipment, and tote bags for each class. From the outset, the instructors were paid a small stipend, more to recognize their commitment than to compensate them for their time. Grace Weatherby reported that:

Each instructor would come into the Center to pack her bag with the supplies needed....For instance, the Wildlife in Winter class required the making of a plaster cast of an animal track to go back to school with the teacher. Plaster of Paris and water plus mixing containers had to be carried, plus identification books so that the students could identify the animal.... Five Rivers Limited came to our rescue and paid for the durable canvas type bags and any supplies that DEC could not pay for. (p. 2.)

Soon the Center was hosting dozens of Kindergarten through eighth grade school classes in its Guided School Program.

The Guided School Program instructors get separate training for each type of class they teach; the number of class topics has varied from seven to twelve over the years. Here DEC Environmental Educator Nancy Payne is training a group who are clearly undeterred by the chill. (Friends of Five Rivers Archives)

A group of GSP instructors from 2001 pose with their DEC trainers: (l. to r.) front row: Craig Thompson, Carolyn Miller, Amy Price, Leda Loux, Anita Sanches, Barb Eames, Karen Jacobs. Second row: unidentified, Mary Lou Riccardo, Anne Snyder, Commie Tilroe, Ted Howell, Noreen Van Cans, Tom Lindsay. Third row: Nicole Donato, Wendy Suozzo, Phyllis Howell, Nancy Payne, George Tilroe, Robin Smith, Dee Strnisa. Back: Dave Peterson. (Friends of Five Rivers Archives)

Importantly, that first winter season set the pattern. GSP classes would be held outdoors. Indoor staging time would be kept to a minimum. Students would be taught to experience and enjoy the outdoors all year round: to see, hear, and touch nature directly.

Grace Weatherby emphasized that when she and Wendy Suozzo started the program
Environmental education was really in its infancy....In 1979 or 80 Jan Foley and I represented FRL and DEC at an Outdoor Education Association weekend in the Catskills, where we gave a program....It was well attended and many of the groups continued to be in touch with Center staff ...to set up similar programs.

One teacher who brought classes to Five Rivers actually decided on a career change as a result. Grade school teacher Nancy Payne was so intrigued by the Center that she accepted a position as environmental educator in 1980. Her knowledge of elementary school children made her an excellent trainer for GSP instructors. Nancy also began recruiting and training "assistant naturalists" and "junior naturalists," adults and students who could help the Center staff with maintaining collections and presenting public programs.

Several teaching shelters were built over the years to facilitate teaching in the rain and snow. This one, donated by the Repass family, is protecting a group of teachers from the sun during a summer training program. (Photo by RA Fogarty)

Herb Repass, addressing a Friends of Five Rivers audience at the event where Wendy Suozzo's picture was added to the Five Rivers Hall of Fame. Also in the front row are Herb's wife Peggy, and their son-in-law Jim Suozzo, flanked by his sons Matt and Chris.

After an initial period under the coordination of Grace Weatherby, Gerry Oakley took on the Guided School Program as part of her duties as FFR/FRL administrator. Gerry did dual duty until 1990. By that time, the Guided School Program had shown sufficient growth to justify a second staff member for the Friends. A position was created for a GSP coordinator, held in succession by Joanne Gwinn (1990-96); Anne Snyder (1996-2002); Wendy Repass Suozzo (2002-2009); and Nancy Conway (2009 to present).

In 2002 things seemed to come full circle. Wendy Repass Suozzo, who had written most of the original GSP lessons and then resigned from her Center staff position in 1983 to raise her children, became available. She was hired as GSP coordinator in 2002, serving until her untimely death from cancer in 2008. With Wendy the GSP, the Friends, and the Center gained not just an employee but a family commitment to support the Center.

In the years of Wendy's involvement and continuing after her death, her family members— parents, siblings, husband, and sons-- have been remarkable patrons of the cause of environmental education. Their contributions have included the half million dollar gift to construct the new Guided School Program building, as well as a gift to construct the teaching shelter at Goose Pond. They have also contributed to the ongoing school bus scholarship program, enabling districts without field trip money to send classes to Five Rivers. They created the Wendy Repass Suozzo Memorial Scholarship for a Bethlehem High School senior who plans to pursue environmental studies. Wendy's husband Jim has been a longtime supporter of the Center, and his son Matt contributes his time and skills to implementing the Friends' website.

Today the Guided School program serves school classes from throughout the region. In the 2011 calendar year, 310 classes were held for a total of approximately 3,959 children. The Guided School Program is currently coordinated by Nancy Conway, hired in 2008. Her skills as an engineer have been invaluable during the planning and construction of the GSP building, and her people skills and hard work have helped with the difficult transition after Wendy Suozzo's death.

Friends' Volunteers: Wherever Needed

The committee structure of Friends of Five Rivers Board of Directors is a good index of the kinds of services volunteers now provide at the center.

○ Accessible Trail Committee: maintains the surface of the handicapped accessible trail;.

○ Annual Meeting Committee: schedules the meeting and speaker;

○ Birdseed Sale Committee: purchases seed in bulk for resale to members;.

○ Fall Festival Committee: works with Center staff to plan and carry out the annual Fall Festival each September, a free event that draws 2000 visitors;

○ Finance/Fund Raising: initiates and oversees financial programs;

○ Greeter Coordinator: schedules volunteers to cover the front desk as needed;

○ Hospitality Committee: provides food and drink for members and volunteers at all events

○ Land Protection Committee: maintains relations with surrounding landowners; explores potential land donations and purchases;

○ Membership Committee: plans and carries out membership recruitment and monthly mailings;

○ Newsletter Editor: publishes quarterly newsletter of Friends of Five Rivers, *Rivers Ramblings*;

○ Nominating Committee: recruits replacements for outgoing Board members and officers;

○ Off-Site Events Committee: provides coverage for a Five Rivers table at public events;

○ Public Relations Committee: issues press releases and develops PR materials;

○ Suozzo Memorial Fund Committee: administers the Wendy Repass Suozzo Memorial Fund;

○ Trail Maintenance Committee: works with the

Nature's Backyard Trail (see map on following page), constructed in 1996 , is a fully accessible paved trail with many enticing features for anyone riding a wheelchair, using a walker, pushing a stroller, or just easily fatigued by walking. There are regularly spaced accessible benches, and (shown here) a Wildlife Garden designed to attract bees and butterflies, and a Pond Garden. An observation platform and a large gazebo enable users to watch birds and enjoy views over Beaver and Heron ponds. (Photos by RA Fogarty)

Center director to maintain Center trails;

o Volunteer Recognition Event Committee: plans and carries out an annual Volunteer Recognition Meeting;

o Website Interface Committee: maintains the Friends of Five Rivers website,
www.FriendsofFiveRivers.org.;

o Wildlife Gardeners: maintain the Wildlife Garden and the Pond Garden.

This is a mind-boggling array of tasks for today's eighteen-member Board. New nominees to the Friends Board are warned that "this is a working board," not simply a policy-making board. Many volunteers and past Board members back up the Board with hundreds of person-hours of commitment each year. Center Director Craig Thompson estimates that the volunteer commitment at the Center is equivalent to three full-time staff members.

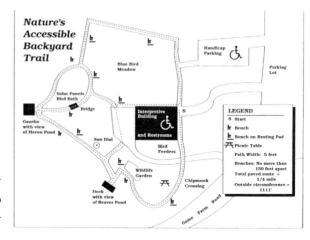

Friends of Five Rivers Newsletter ~ www.friendsoffiverivers.org   Spring 2012

Environmental Achievement Awards

Share your Five Rivers' memories and stories.

The Friends of Five Riv...

The Friends of Five Rivers' first annual Environmental Achievement Awards were given at a reception on April 20th at the Albany Country Club. Over 90 volunteers, board members, staff and DEC staff attended the reception.

The Environmental Achievement awards honor outstanding, innovative and creative environmentalists who have a positive impact on the environment and Five Rivers.

Gerry started volunteering in 1977 when her youngest child started

ronmental Education Center. Grace retired from the Friends of Five Rivers in 1981.

Geraldine Oakley served as Program Coordinator of the Friends for twelve years and continues to volunteer with the Friends . Her dedication to Five Rivers is well known and greatly appreciated.

In the early days of the Center, The Tributary newsletter was a joint venture of the DEC staff and the Friends. Later The Tributary became confined to reporting on Center programs, and the Friends began to issue its own newsletter, Rivers Ramblings, for its membership. When DEC stopped funding print newsletters, the Friends began enclosing the Center's program list in Ramblings, as well as posting it on the Friends' website. (Friends of Five Rivers Archives)

An important part of Friends of Five Rivers' role has been to provide funding for activities and equipment that are central to the mission of the Center. For example, Friends funding pays for the snowshoes that make outdoor trail walks possible year-round. In 2008 a school bus scholarship program was started to pay for busing for classes from school districts that had no field trip funds. The handicapped accessible binoculars in the gazebo came from Friends income. The gazebo itself was a gift celebrating the 50th anniversary of the Ganeys, since Santa Ganey volunteered for many years. In fact, many people send memorial gifts to Friends of Five Rivers to recognize the love of a friend for the Center, and those gifts go to meet program needs. (Photos by RA Fogarty)

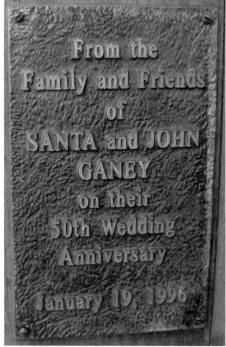

From the
Family and Friends
of
SANTA and JOHN
GANEY
on their
50th Wedding
Anniversary

January 19, 1996

Friends of Five Rivers holds an annual volunteer recognition event, with a speaker on an environmental topic, refreshments, and a gift for each volunteer—usually a plant, appropriately enough! (Photo by RA Fogarty)

Candidates for the Board of the Friends of Five Rivers are frequently told "This is a working board." Each member takes on a volunteer commitment at the center and usually chairs a committee supervising other volunteers, in addition to attending monthly board meetings (shown here). (Photo by RA Fogarty)

Board member Phyllis Hathaway and Board President Rich Bader work on an activity at a Board retreat in June 2011. Friends of Five Rivers' Board periodically revisits its mission and goals to check for current relevance. Nine-year term limits for the Board ensure that new voices and new ideas are heard regularly. (Photo by RA Fogarty)

Recognition

On occasion the Friends of Five Rivers has been singled out for community recognition. In 1984, Board president Margaret Hay accepted an award on behalf of Five Rivers Limited from the Mohawk-Hudson Community Foundation. In 1996 the group was recognized as an "Environmental Partner" by DEC for its land protection efforts. In 1999 the group received the Governors Community Service Award in recognition for having "for over 25 years provided people power and financial support" to Five Rivers.

Top right: Margaret Hay and Gerry Oakley accepted a Mohawk Hudson Community Foundation Award on behalf of the Friends in 1984. (Friends of Five Rivers Archives)

Above: Friends of Five Rivers was recognized as a DEC Environmental Partner in 1996. (Friends of Five Rivers Archives)

Bottom right: Craig Thompson, Leda Loux, Dan Lewis, and Peter Keitel accepted a Governor's Service Award for Five Rivers Limited from Lieutenant Governor Mary Donohue in 1999. (Friends of Five Rivers Archives)

More commonly, however, the group tends to operate under the public's radar. A good example is the Five Rivers Fall Festival, for which the Friends provide a large percentage of the planning and organizing. Publicity; food and beverages; musical entertainment; trail hikes; children's crafts and puppet shows; sales of plants, books, and baked goods; set-up and clean-up: all involve months of organization and planning by a large volunteer committee, plus dozens of volunteers who serve on the day of the festival.

A Permanent Commitment?

Five Rivers Environmental Education Center has seemingly risen from its own ashes over and over. Other centers have struggled and continue to struggle with the threat of extermination. Clearly the existence of an active, vocal, fearless, and committed citizen support group makes a difference. However, the existence of an all-volunteer group like Friends of Five Rivers always has an underlying vulnerability. Current Friends Board president Richard Bader likes to point out that Five Rivers hosts approximately 100,000 visitors a year, yet Friends of Five Rivers has only about 750 members.

Will new generations of people continue to find the mission of Friends of Five Rivers compelling? Will they be willing to contribute the time and effort to serve as Board members and volunteers? Will they understand the fragility of the Center, now surrounded by suburban development, and make the commitment to protecting it?

These are not rhetorical questions. The history of Five Rivers shows that, time and again, individual citizens must step forward if this special place is to survive. In the words of anthropologist Margaret Mead: "A small group of thoughtful people could change the world. Indeed, it is the only thing that ever has."

Photo by Morgan Gmelch

Chapter 9 Resources

Budliger, Robert. Review of *"Five Rivers History"*. January, 2012

Capital Area Environmental Education Center at Delmar (proposed). (Undated proposal and proposed map, from the files of Five Rivers Limited.)

Certificate of Incorporation of Five Rivers Limited Under Section 402 of the Not-for-Profit Corporation Law, February 3, 1972. (From the files of Five Rivers Limited).

Five Rivers Limited. *Board Minutes: 1972-1993*. (From the files of Five Rivers Limited.)

Loux, Leda. Review of *Five Rivers History Draft*. January 2012.

Mapes, Alan. Comments on *"Five Rivers History"*. February 22, 2012.

Oakley, Gerry. Comments on *"Five Rivers History."* January 25, 2012

Passer, Jerry. *Assorted memoranda*. In *Board Minutes: 1972-1993*. (From the files of Five Rivers Limited.)

Payne, Nancy. Comments on *"Five Rivers History."* February, 2012

Smolinsky, John. *FFR – Friends Beginnings*, (Summary essay on Friends of Five Rivers establishment and accomplishments), 2009.

25th Birthday Celebration, June 14, 1997. (Invitational flyer from the files of Five Rivers Limited.)

Weatherby, Grace E. Comments on *"Five Rivers History."* January 28, 2012.

Weatherby, Grace E. History of Five Rivers Limited Guided Program (Memorandum, 1988.)

Photo by RA Fogarty

CHAPTER 10

INTO THE FUTURE

Jackson's obituary for the American frontier was only partly accurate;
one frontier did disappear, but a second one followed,
in which Americans romanticized, exploited, protected, and destroyed nature.
Now that frontier, which existed in the family farm,
the woods at the end of the road, the national parks, and our hearts—
is itself disappearing or changing beyond recognition.

Richard Louv
Last Child in the Woods
2006

Truly, time marches on, and we walk to the beat of its drum, always confronting the new challenges that time brings. At Five Rivers, we walk in the footprints of the mastodon, perhaps hunted to extinction by early man. We walk in the footprints of the Mohican, forced out of ancestral hunting grounds by the new reality of commercial competition. We walk in the footprints of the farmer, turning up arrowheads with his plow, unaware that the time for farming this land would be limited. We walk in the footprints of the CCC worker, sweating to build a barn for the breeding of game birds, little knowing that the pastime of game hunting itself might disappear. We walk in the footprints of wide-eyed children who came to learn about creatures that share their world, creatures whose habitat was already shrinking in the face of suburban development.

At the time of this book's publication, Five Rivers Environmental Education Center faces new challenges. Construction of a long-awaited building from which to base the teaching of children,

Photo by Michael J. Fogarty

balked by many delays, is nearing completion. New York State's deficit has forced a severe staff reduction at the Center, and other centers have actually been closed. Encroaching development threatens to make the Center's permeable boundaries too accessible to humans for the health and safety of the many other species that live here.

A generation or two ago, a child might have had a special, secret place in the natural world— a big rock out in a field, a particular circle of trees at the back of the yard, a bit of wilderness across the tracks or at the end of the street. It was a place to be alone, or to share with a best friend, a sanctuary in the outdoors. Today's children are less likely to have such places, for reasons worn threadbare by discussion.

The contributors to this book share a faith that Five Rivers will persist and thrive, because for so many of its friends it is an irreplaceable and timeless "special place."

APPENDIX

FIVE RIVERS "HALL OF FAME"

Initiated by Center Director Craig Thompson, the Hall of Fame collection of photographs and biographical notes in the Five Rivers Center classroom has grown year by year. Presented here in the order in which they were inducted are the thirty members of the Hall of Fame as of summer of 2012.

ROBERT DARROW

Wildlife Research Laboratory, 1931-1988

Bob Darrow began an illustrious career in conservation during the summer of 1931 while working on the storied Connecticut Hill grouse survey. Through 1942, Mr. Darrow also conducted field research in the winter mortality of white-tailed deer in the Adirondacks. In recognition of his outstanding talent for organizing field research, Mr. Darrow was appointed Supervisor of Game Research at the Wildlife Research Laboratory, where he co-authored the seminal study ***The Ruffed Grouse***. In 1954, he was appointed Editor of DEC's research organ, ***The New York Fish and Game Journal***, a position he held for nearly 35 years.

DR. GARDINER BUMP

Delmar Experimental Game Farm
Superintendent, 1933-1948

Dr. Bump began his state service in 1926 working under Dr. A. A. Allen on the famous Connecticut Hill grouse survey. The first Superintendent of the Delmar Game Farm, Dr. Bump supervised a range of game propagation and research projects from 1933-1948, focusing primarily on upland game birds. In 1947, Dr. Bump and his associates published their voluminous findings in the seminal study *The Ruffed Grouse*, which remains perhaps the most comprehensive study of any game bird ever undertaken. Dr. Bump went on to further distinguish himself in international game bird research studying grouse, pheasant, partridge and quail species on five continents for the US Fish and Wildlife Service from 1949-1970.

ALBERT LANOUE

Civilian Conservation Corps Camp S-72
1934-1936

Albert Lanoue was a member of the site's Civilian Conservation Corps Camp S-72 from 1934-36, specializing in fleet management. In addition to maintaining the Company's extensive inventory of rolling stock, Albert was responsible for driving the Company ambulance, crew truck, dump truck and other service vehicles. The Company had no construction vehicles; all work was done by hand. Albert grew up in Cohoes, a neighbor of Captain Joseph J. Ruddy, the Company Commander. Like many CCC enrollees, Albert put his CCC training to good use, thereafter working for American Locomotive in Schenectady, retiring in 1968.

BERT POLAND

Civilian Conservation Corps Camp S-72 and
Delmar Experimental Game Farm
1934-1938

Bert Poland was a member the site's Civilian Conservation Corps Camp S-72, one of only three CCC enlistees hired on by the Game Farm. In 1934-35, Bert helped to develop our system of duck ponds along the Vlomankill, including laying the stone and earthen berms for Beaver Pond and Heron Pond, work all done by hand. Bert also enjoyed working with wildlife at the Game Farm, where he served until 1938.

LLEWELLYN "TARZAN" BAKER

Civilian Conservation Corps Camp S-72 and
Delmar Experimental Game Farm
1934-1963

A member of the site's Civilian Conservation Corps Camp S-72 from 1934-36, Tarzan was involved in the initial site work at the Delmar Experimental Game Farm, including construction of Heron and Beaver Ponds. He also took readily to helping out with propagation activity at the Game Farm, working with all manner of wildlife, thus earning his endearing nickname. Because of his work ethic and affinity for the outdoors, he was hired at the Game Farm when the CCC camp closed in 1936. He served as Assistant Game Farm Foreman until 1963, when he left to become Foreman of Switzkill Farm, a private game farm.

STEPHEN C. FORDHAM

Delmar Experimental Game Farm
1938-1972

Steve Fordham devoted his working career to the Delmar Experimental Game Farm. He was appointed Foreman of the Game Farm upon graduation from Cornell University in 1938, and continued in that role until 1972. Mr. Fordham took great pride in overseeing the Game Farm's legendary propagation programs with upland game birds and waterfowl. Under Mr. Fordham's aegis, the Game Farm produced as many as 100,000 game birds a year for distribution throughout New York State. With the closing of the Game Farm in 1972, Mr. Fordham continued as a Conservation Department pilot, retiring in 1979.

WILLIAM SEVERINGHAUS

Wildlife Research Laboratory
Principal Wildlife Biologist, 1938-1977

A Principal Wildlife Biologist at the Delmar Wildlife Research Laboratory, Bill began working during summers in the late 1930s under Gardiner Bump on the famous Connecticut Hill grouse survey. Coming to Delmar in 1938, Bill captained a variety of research projects involving white tailed deer, where his seminal studies of deer food habits and age determination revolutionized wildlife management nation-wide and helped establish NYS DEC as a leader in the conservation profession. Techniques developed under Bill's leadership are still critical tools in the wildlife manager's repertoire today.

DON FOLEY

Wildlife Research Laboratory
1938-1977

One of the original grouse surveyors on the seminal Connecticut Hill study, Don Foley was a member of the vaunted Cornell Class of 1940, many of whom went on to successful careers with the Conservation Department. Don's state service spanned 35 years, most notably as a Supervising Wildlife Biologist at the Wildlife Research Laboratory, where he specialized in wetlands and waterfowl management. A man before his time, Don was one of the first to call public attention to wetlands destruction and degradation, and helped lay the foundation for the Department's wetlands acquisition plan. Wildlife managers still refer to the comprehensive regional waterfowl management guides which he authored.

DR. E. L. CHEATUM

Wildlife Research Laboratory
1939-1968

Dr. E.L. Cheatum was one of the state's first wildlife pathologists, initially operating out of the site's former CCC infirmary in 1939, moving into Delmar's new Wildlife Research Laboratory in 1941. Doc Cheatum conducted groundbreaking research in wildlife diseases and parasites, specializing in pheasants, rabbits, ducks, deer and muskrats. He served DEC for 30 years, becoming Assistant Director of the Division of Fish and Game in 1959, and its Director in 1964.

JOSEPH DELL

Wildlife Research Laboratory
Supervising Wildlife Biologist, 1941-1979

A Supervising Wildlife Biologist at the Delmar Wildlife Resources Laboratory, Joe oversaw a variety of small game research projects, most notably dealing with cottontail rabbits and both snowshoe and European hare. In response to an alarming state-wide decline in snowshoe hare, Joe conducted a comprehensive field study near the Jones Barn to determine the feasibility of propagating hare in the game farm environment.

CLINT BISHOP

Delmar Experimental Game Farm
1948-1970

A Delmar Game Farm Conservation Aide with a special knack for wildlife exhibition, Clint Bishop established a menagerie in 1948 that was known far and wide as the Delmar Zoo. Billed as "the only place where you can see most all of the important species of the state", the zoo was the site's first public outreach initiative and established our standing as a vibrant educational institution and community resource.

GENE PARKS

Wildlife Research Laboratory
1949-1986

Gene Parks served the Department for 37 years, spending most of his career as a Principal Wildlife Biologist at Delmar's Wildlife Research Laboratory. Trained in pharmacy, Gene oversaw a state-wide rabies research and control program during the '50s and '60s. He went on to supervise DEC's initial implementation of the Fish and Wildlife Management Act, retiring in 1986 as the Assistant Bureau Chief of the Division of Fish and Wildlife.

STU FREE

Wildlife Research Laboratory
1956-1986

Stu Free served DEC in many leadership capacities for nearly 30 years. He was the big game project leader, and later Supervising Wildlife Biologist, at Delmar's Wildlife Research Laboratory from 1956-1972. Stu helped author the Fish and Wildlife Resources Report for the Temporary State Commission on the Catskills in 1974, and was DEC's Chief of the Bureau of Wildlife from 1975-1986, a decade of exceptional success in both game and non-game management programs.

EARL WESTERVELT

Division of Educational Services

1957-1975

A member of the celebrated Connecticut Hill gang, "Westy" came to Conservation Education from the Division of Fish and Wildlife in 1957. He administered the Department's Conservation Camps and served as the Senior Editor of the renowned ***Conservationist*** magazine through 1970, when he became Director of the Division of Conservation Education, and subsequently Assistant Director of the Division of Educational Services. Mr. Westervelt first envisioned a state-wide network of regional conservation education centers, and played a pivotal role in establishing the Department's ***Five Rivers Environmental Education Center*** in 1972.

EDWARD GERVAIS

Delmar Operations

1962-present

Ed Gervais came to the Game Farm in 1962 as a General Mechanic, working for the Division of Conservation Education. In addition to performing maintenance and groundskeeping duties for what was then known as "The Delmar Zoo," Ed soon found himself involved in everything from exhibit construction to wildlife rehabilitation. With the closing of the Game Farm and Zoo in 1972, Ed played a key role in converting the facility to environmental education. Boasting a career that spans 5 decades, Ed is the longest tenured Delmar Operations staff member ever.

ERIC AND BERNICE LEIGHTON

Five Rivers Limited
Founding Members, 1971-1980

Due to their long standing involvement in local environmental affairs, Eric and Bernice Leighton were invited to attend the initial organizational meeting of Five Rivers Limited in October 1971. During Five Rivers Limited's formative year, the Leightons hosted many Board meetings at their home, and, before the Education Center was established in June 1972, commonly fielded the whole gamut of wildlife inquiries on their home phone. The Leightons were active Board members for nearly a decade and enjoyed nature walking at Five Rivers for many years thereafter. Eric was active in the Bethlehem Sportsmen's Club and Bernice in the League of Women Voters, and they were Charter Members of the Audubon Society of the Capital Region.

THE HONORABLE ERASTUS CORNING II

Five Rivers Limited
Board Member, 1971-1981

While serving as Mayor of Albany, the Honorable Erastus Corning II was an active and influential member of Five Rivers Limited during the initial stages of its development, and served on its Board as Treasurer. The Mayor especially played a pivotal role in favorably resolving a plan to close Five Rivers Center in 1980. An avid sportsman, Mayor Corning took a deep personal interest in all the research and education activities at DEC's Delmar site and facilitated a wide range of projects, from land acquisition to specimen collection. Along with his hunting buddy, Dr. Bump, Mayor Corning helped found the Capital District Chapter of the Ruffed Grouse Society.

ROBERT BUDLIGER

Five Rivers Environmental Education Center
Director, 1973-1978

Five Rivers' first Director, Bob developed the education and information regime and management protocols which still form the foundation of the Center's work plan today. Drawing on his experience in the National Park Service and as a high school biology teacher, Bob turned the former Delmar Game Farm into a model environmental education facility, a benchmark to which similar facilities would be compared. In recognition of Bob's leadership, the National Park Service named Five Rivers Center a *National Environmental Study Area* in 1977, the first and only such area in the state. Bob went on to become NYS DEC's Chief of the Bureau of Environmental Education and continued to bring state-wide and national acclaim to the Bureau.

ALAN MAPES

Five Rivers Environmental Education Center
Environmental Educator 1974-1977
Director, 1978-1995

Alan was one of the many Cornell alums who over the years have brought both scholarly rigor and progressive vision to DEC's Division of Public Affairs. A gadget-guy from the get-go, Alan's facility with technology brought the Center, and later the entire Bureau, into the electronic age. An avid birder, Alan firmly established Five Rivers as the Capital Region's home office for bird education, bird watching and citizen science. Dubbed "Mr. Bluebird" by the Times Union, Alan set up an extensive "nest box trail" in the early '80s which is still highly successful today. In 1995, Alan went on serve as DEC's Chief of the Bureau of Environmental Education, where he captained an era of growth and innovation until his retirement in 2006.

WENDY REPASS SUOZZO

Five Rivers Environmental Education Center
Senior Environmental Educator, 1977-1983
Friends of Five Rivers School Program Coordinator, 2002 - 2008

As the Center's Senior Educator, Wendy oversaw the development of the guided school program. Her early advocacy of immersing visitors within nature remains the hallmark of Center activity today. A stickler for detail, she held staff to the highest standards of professionalism and scientific accuracy, earning Center programs a well-deserved reputation for quality. Vacating her post in 1983 to start her family, she returned as the Friends of Five Rivers' School Program Coordinator in 2002, directing the very program which she helped initiate 25 years earlier. Wendy dedicated her career to helping others to see sermons in stones, and to understand the profound spiritual power of the special place she loved so dearly.

LORRAINE WHITING

Five Rivers Environmental Education Center
1977 - 2009

Five Rivers' first and only Administrative Professional, Lori played a major role in developing and overseeing every aspect of Center management and operation. In addition to performing the full gamut of traditional "office manager" tasks, Lori developed exceptional expertise in handling all manner of inquiry related to nuisance, orphaned or injured wildlife. A local town historian in her other life, Lori brought an uncanny research acumen and organizational rigor to Center programming, producing reference material, interpretive script, exhibit layouts, publications - even conducting public programs. She deftly exploited the tumultuous changes which technology brought to her profession during her 30 year tenure.

GERALDINE OAKLEY

Five Rivers Limited
1977 - present

For 30 years, Gerry Oakley has served Five Rivers Limited in a variety of key capacities, some simultaneously. Gerry started out as a volunteer photographer in 1977, later becoming a member of FRL's first Volunteer Instructor corps in 1978. In 1981, Gerry became FRL's Administrator and School Program Coordinator, multi-tasking for over a decade in these capacities. She led the guided lesson program through a period of tremendous growth, while overseeing a five-fold increase in FRL's operating budget. Many instructional frameworks and quality control practices developed under Gerry's aegis are still in use today. Gerry has continued to serve the Friends group as a volunteer since her "retirement" in 1993.

MARY LOU RICCARDO

Friends of Five Rivers
Volunteer Instructor, 1978 - 2010

Mary Lou had been a Volunteer Instructor since the very beginning of the Guided School Program, teaching over 950 field classes, the most of any docent. A stickler for scientific accuracy, she meticulously researched series of species accounts as a reference for the instructor corps, and developed a handy "flip and show" guide for use afield, both of which are still widely used today. Over many years Mary Lou was able to amass a remarkable collection of maple syrup antiques and artifacts which she graciously displayed in the Visitor Center each spring. A dedicated wildlife rehabilitator for twenty years and founder of the Wildlife Rehabilitation and Education Network, Mary Lou brought a knowledgeable and caring presence to all her education activities.

NANCY PAYNE

Five Rivers Environmental Education Center
Environmental Educator, 1980 - 2010

During her illustrious career, Nancy developed many cutting-edge initiatives. In 1985, she started an Assistant Naturalist program, providing real-time training for aspiring interpreters. Her spin-off Student Naturalist Program has given budding interpreters as young as 10 meaningful hands-on work experience. For over 27 years, her acclaimed Summer Family Program has strengthened the parent/child bond through a shared connection to nature. In 1996, Nancy developed a stones-and-bones loan program called Tails By Mail. But her best work was in her teaching. A certified school teacher and an accomplished story teller, she could hold an audience in the palm of her hand. The many staff and volunteers whom she touched far and wide will long remember and fondly consult her exceptional methodology.

DR. ROBERT AND ELEANOR ALEXANDER

Five Rivers Limited
1981-1990

Bob and Eleanor Alexander served Five Rivers Limited in various key capacities throughout the 1980s, providing leadership and vision during a period of robust growth at Five Rivers. Bob served for 9 years on the Board, and was its President from 1986-1988. He was active as a Volunteer Instructor and oversaw the development of the Center's first Master Plan in 1985. Eleanor was one of the Center's first Volunteer Greeters and her welcoming presence at the Information Desk became a fixture on weekends at the Visitor Center.

BILL AND ELEANOR HAYWOOD

Five Rivers Limited
1981-2003

Bill and Eleanor Haywood served Five Rivers Limited in several key capacities for over 20 years. They served on the Board throughout the '80s, and together helped guide the Center through a heady period of innovation and growth. In 1982, Eleanor established a cadre of volunteer Greeters to staff the Information Desk on weekends, and was active on FRL's education, membership and newsletter committees. An avid outdoorsman eager to share his passion for nature, Bill was a fixture at the Information Desk on weekends.

HANK DECENZO

Delmar Operations
Conservation Operations Maintenance Assistant
1984-2009

Hank Decenzo's career spanned a quarter century of public service. From 1984-87, Hank worked on the field crew stationed at the Delmar working circle. He was re-assigned to DEC's Cherry Plain substation in 1987, where, among other duties, he monitored the remediation of the Dewey Loeffel landfill. He returned to Delmar in 1995, working with field crews until 1998, thereafter on the Five Rivers maintenance crew. A respected and highly capable gadget-guy, Hank was especially adept at trouble-shooting mechanical systems. His many constructive suggestions improved site management, often saving time and money.

LEDA LOUX

Friends of Five Rivers
1984 - 2011

Leda's long and memorable tenure began in 1984 as a some-time Volunteer Instructor while her boys were growing up. In 1993, she began a highly productive 18-year stint as the Friends' Administrator, ably managing an ever-growing ledger of fiscal, developmental and programmatic responsibilities. The many enduring milestone projects accomplished under her guidance have advanced every aspect of Center growth and development, most notably: coordinating the development of Nature's Accessible Backyard Trail; organizing the Friends' acquisition of the Bishop and Foresman properties; administering grants in support of mission-critical programs; and managing expanded Guided School Program, intern and volunteer initiatives.

ANITA SANCHEZ

Five Rivers Environmental Education Center
Summer Intern 1973
Senior Environmental Educator 1984-2010

Anita started at Five Rivers as a teenager in the summer of 1973, when there was 1 desk, 1 phone and staff meetings were conducted at a picnic table. After graduation from Vassar, she served on the staff at DEC's Stonykill Center, then at DEC's Rogers Center, before rejoining staff at Five Rivers in 1984. A staunch proponent of direct contact with nature, she championed the "hands on" approach – the experience is the message. In 2005, Anita developed an innovative classroom program for inner city schools which continues today. A treasure trove of wildflower lore, she published an inspiring tribute to the lowly dandelion in 2006. She was less enthusiastic about other non-native species, mustering all hands in protracted war with invasives such as garlic mustard, water chestnut and phragmites. Always passionate about least toxic alternatives, she brought many green practices and programs to Five Rivers.

DIANA (DEE) STRNISA

Friends of Five Rivers
Volunteer Instructor 1981-1999
Five Rivers Environmental Education Center
Environmental Educator, 2000-2010

A well-respected reptile and amphibian expert, Dee served as a dedicated Volunteer Instructor for nearly two decades. She joined Five Rivers staff in 2000, overseeing the state-wide implementation of Project WET (Water Education for Teachers). Dee started Five Rivers' participation in several citizen science initiatives which continue today: Hudson River Snapshot Day; World Water Monitoring Day; Frogwatch monitoring and Vlomankill bio-assessment. Dee never turned down requests for her time and enjoyed enthralling audiences far and wide with her eye-popping presentations, always embellished with live creepy crawly specimens from her own menagerie. She especially enjoyed sharing her passion for wildlife at sportsman's shows and special events, reaching tens of thousands annually.

BIBLIOGRAPHY

Adams, Arthur G. *The Hudson Throught the Years (2ⁿᵈ Edition)*. New York: Fordham University Press, 1996.

Alsheimer, Charles J. "Forty Years of Deer Research," *Deer and Deer Hunting*. February 1983,: 33-37.

Armstrong, Shirley. "Delmar Game Farm Planning 'Native Setting' for Stock. *Times Union,* Albany, NY, August 26, 1970

Baker, George. Interview by Dan Ruge. Albany, NY: Five Rivers Archives. June 23, 1993.

Baker, Llewellyn. Personal Writings. Albany, NY: Five Rivers Archives, undated.

Baker, Llewelyn (Earl). Correspondence with Nancy Payne,

Baldridge, Kenneth W. *The Civilian Conservation Corps;* Utah History Encyclopedia. July 1, 2006. http://www.media.utah.edu/UHE/c/CIVCONCOR.html

Basser, T.J. "Mahican." In *The Handbook of North American Indians*. 15:198-212. Washington, DC: Government Printing Office, 1978.

Bennett, Allison. *More Times Remembered*. Salem, MS: Higginson Book Company, 1987.

Bennett, Allison. *Times Remembered*. Salem, MS: Higginson Book Company, 1984.

Berlin, Ira and Harris, Leslie M. (Eds.) *Slavery In New York*. New York, NY, The New Press, 2005.

Bethlehem Historical Association. *Records of the People of the Town of Bethlehem, Albany County, New York: 1698 – 1880*. Interlaken, NY: Heart of the Lakes Publishing, 1982.

Bethlehem History Committee; Brewer, Floyd I. (Sr. Ed.) *Bethlehem Revisited: A Bicentennial Story: 1793 – 1993*. Town of Bethlehem, NY: Bethlehem Bicentennial Commission, 1993.

Budliger, Robert. Review of "Five Rivers History." Delmar, NY, Five Rivers Archives: January 2012.

Bump, Gardiner. *Pheasant Rearing.* Delmar, NY: Five Rivers Archives, undated.

Burke, Thomas E. *Mohawk Frontier: The Dutch Community of Schenectady, NY 1661-1710.* Ithaca, NY: Cornell University Press, 1991.

Capital Area Environmental Education Center at Delmar (proposed). (Undated proposal and proposed map, from the files of Five Rivers Limited.)

Cartledge, Jerry. "Delmar Lab Is Center of Huge Wildlife Research Program," *Times Union*, Albany, NY, Sunday, March 1, 1959 (Section E, pp. 4 and 6.)

Certificate of Incorporation of Five Rivers Limited Under Section 402 of the Not-for-Profit Corporation Law, February 3, 1972. (From the files of Five Rivers Limited).

Christman, Henry. *Tin Horns and Calico: A Decisive Episode in the Emergence of Democracy.* Cornwallville, NY: Hope Farm Press, 1978.

_____. *Civilian Conservation Corps.* Maryland Department of Natural Resources. June 25, 2006. http://www.dnr.state.md.us/publiclands/ccchistory.html

Clyne, Patricia Edwards. "Chapter 12: Climbing the Indian Ladder Trail," in *Hudson Valley Tales and Trails.* Woodstock, NY: The Overlook Press, 1990.

Collamer and Associates, Inc. *Stage 1A and Stage 1B Cultural Resource Investigations for Five Rivers Environmental Education Center, Wildlife Resources Center, Delmar Waterline Project.* (114 Gardner Hill, East Nassau, NY 12062) September 30, 1992

Constitution of the State of New York, Article XVI

Dell, Joe. Interview by Dan Ruge, Albany NY: Five Rivers Archives, June 8, 1993.

Dietz, Donald. *Five Rivers Environmental Education Center and the CCCs*, June 25, 2006. http://www.geocities.com/ccchistory/270.html

Duncan, Dayton and Burns, Ken. *The National Parks: America's Best Idea—An Illustrated History.* New York: Alfred A Knopf, 2009

Duncan, Dayton and Burns, Ken. *The National Parks: America's Best Idea.* New York: Alfred A. Knopf, 2009.

Dunn, Shirley W. and Bennett, Allison P. *Dutch Architecture Near Albany: the Polgreen Photographs.* Fleischmanns, NY: Purple Mountain Press, 1996.

Dunn, Shirley. *The Mohican World, 1680-1750.* Fleischmanns, NY: Purple Mountain Press, 2000.

Dunn, Shirley. *The Mohicans and Their Land, 1609-1730.* Fleischmanns, NY: Purple Mountain Press, 1994.

Eisenstadt, Peter (Ed.) *The Encyclopedia of New York State.* Syracuse, NY Syracuse University Press, 2005

Ellis, David M. et al. *A History of New York State.* Ithaca, NY: NYS Historical Association with Cornell University Press, 1957

Faragher, John Mack, et al. *Out of Many: A History of the American People (5th Edition).* Pearson/Prentice Hall: Upper Saddle River, NJ, 2009

Five Rivers Limited. *Board Minutes: 1972-1993.* (From the files of Five Rivers Limited.)

Five Rivers Limited. *Five Rivers Environmental Education Center Master Plan: Prepared for the Department of Environmental Conservation by the Directors of Five Rivers Limited, Inc., in Consultation with the Staff of Five Rivers Center.* March 1, 1987 (From the files of Five Rivers Limited.)

Five Rivers Limited. *Five Rivers Master Plan: 1993 Update.* (From the files of Five Rivers Limited.)

Fortey, Richard. *Earth: An Intimate History.* NY: Alfred A. Knopf, 2004

Gallman, Norman J. "Delmar Game Farm Is Exciting Wildlife 'Orphanage'." *Union Star*, December 15, 1962.

_____ "A Game Crop is a Community Asset: New York State Experimental Game Farm." *Knickerbocker News*, Albany, NY, Monday, April 17, 1939, (Section 2, p. 1).

Gregg, Arthur B. *Old Helleberg.* Guilderland Center, NY: Guilderland Historical Society, 1975.

Grondahl, Paul. "Loons' Water Turns Deadly," *Times Union*. October 27, 2006, (Section A, pp. 1 and 8.)

Hartgen Archaeological Associates, Inc. *The Tate Site: Phase III Data Retrieval Investigation*. (1744 Washington Ave. Extension, Rensselaer, NY 12144) March, 2002.

Hartgen Archaeological Associates, Inc. *Archaeological Field Reconnaisance for NYDEC*. (1744 Washington Ave. Extension, Rensselaer, NY 12144) March 1999.

_____ "Help for the Hunter," *People and Places Magazine,* November 1956: 8-10.

Isachsen, Y.W. et al. (Eds.) *Geology of New York: A Simplified Account (2nd Edition)*. Albany, NY: New York State Museum: Education Leaflet # 28, 2000

Jennings, Francis. "Dutch and Swedish Indian Policies." In *The Handbook of North American Indians*. 4:13-19. Washington, DC: Government Printing Office, 1988

Kim, Sung Bok. *Landlord and Tenant in Colonial New York: Manorial Society, 1664-1775*. Chapel Hill, NC: University of North Carolina Press, 1978

_____ "Science, Life." *Knickerbocker News,* Albany, NY, Tuesday, April 18, 1939, (Second section, p. 1)

Kobrin, David. *The Black Minority in Early New York*. Albany, NY: New York State American Revolution Bicentennial Commission, 1975.

Landing, Ed. *Fossils and "Deep Time" in New York*. Albany, NY: New York State Museum, 2004.

Leopold, Aldo. *A Sand County Almanac*. New York: Ballantine Books, 1970.

Loux, Leda. Review of *Five Rivers History Draft*. Delmar, NY: Five Rivers Archives, January 2012.

Mapes, Alan. Comments on *"Five Rivers History"*. Delmar, NY: Five Rivers Archives, February 22, 2012.

New Scotland Historical Association. *New Scotland Township*. Charleston, SC: Arcadia Publishing, 2000.

New York State Dept of Environmental Conservation. *Five Rivers Environmental Education Center: Draft Unit Management Plan*. Albany County: Towns of New Scotland and Bethlehem, February 2007.

Nicholls, Steve. *Paradise Found: Nature in America at the Time of Discovery.* Chicago, IL: University of Chicago Press, 2009

NYS Department of Environmental Conservation. *Five Rivers Environmental Education Center: Draft Unit Management Plan: Albany Country, Towns of New Scotland and Bethlehem.* February 2007.

NYS Office of General Services. *Program Report: Study to provide a Master Plan: Five Rivers Environmental Education Center, 56 Game Farm Road, Project No. S1469.* July 1, 2005.

O'Connor, Grace. "He Talks of His Animals with Affection." *Times Union*, February 9, 1970.

Oakley, Gerry. Comments on *"Five Rivers History."* Delmar, NY: Five Rivers Archives, January, 2012

Oliver, Merle. Interviewed by RoseAnne Fogarty, February 2011

Pankin, Elle. "Game Farm Future Debated as Delmar "Zoo" Is Closed," *Times Union*, Albany, NY, Sunday, October 10, 1971, Feature Section, p.1.

Passer, Jerry. *Assorted memoranda.* In *Board Minutes: 1972-1993.* (From the files of Five Rivers Limited.)

Payne, Nancy. Comments on *"Five Rivers History."* Delmar, NY: Five Rivers Archives, February, 2012

Peterson, Ray. "Wildlife 'lab' at Delmar Ready—to Minute Detail; To Be Dedicated Friday," *The Knickerbocker News,* Albany, NY, Wednesday, Sept. 24, 1941, (Section A, p. 14)

Ruttenber, E.M. *Indian Tribes of Hudson's River to 1700.* Saugerties, NY: Hope Farm Press (2nd edition reprint, original 1872), 1998

Smolinsky, John. *FFR – Friends Beginnings*, (Summary essay on Friends of Five Rivers establishment and accomplishments), 2009.

_____ "State Game Farm at Delmar Speeds Wild Bird Tests to Supply Hunters in Fall with Pheasants and Duck" *Knickerbocker News*, Albany, NY, Sunday, June 30, 1937, (Section 1, p. 2?).

Stradling, David. *The Nature of New York: An Environmental History of the Empire State.* Ithaca, NY: Cornell University Press, 2010.

Thompson, Craig. "Force for Nature: 75 Years Later: The Legacy of the Civilian Conservation Corps," *New York State Conservationist,* February 2008, pp. 30-36.

Thompson, Ida. *National Audubon Society Field Guide to North American Fossils.* NY: Alfred A. Knopf, 1995

Titus, Robert. *The Catskills in the Ice Age.* Fleischmanns, NY: Purple Mountain Press, 1990

25th Birthday Celebration, June 14, 1997. (Invitational flyer from the files of Five Rivers Limited.)

_____ "2 Charged in Killing of Deer." *Knickerbocker News.* Albany, Tuesday, Dec. 3, 1968. Van Der Donck, Adriaen. *A Description of the New Nethelands.* Syracuse, NY: Syracuse University Press (published in Dutch in 1653, translated to English by Jeremiah Johnson c. 1841), 1968.

Van Diver, Bradford B. *Field Guide: Upstate New York.* (K/H Geology Field Guide Series) Toronto: Kendall/Hunt Publishing Company, 1980

Van Diver, Bradford B. *Roadside Geology of New York.* Missoula, MT: Mountain Press Publishing Company, 1985.

Weatherby, Grace E. Comments on *"Five Rivers History."* Delmar, NY: Five Rivers Archives, January 28, 2012.

Weishampel, David B. and Young, Luther. *Dinosaurs of the East Coast.* Baltimore: Johns Hopkins University Press, 1996.

Wilkin, Jeff. "Forgotten Contribution: Young men in Civilian Conservation Corps toiled long and hard beautifying American during the Great Depression." *The Daily Gazette,* Tuesday, Oct. 2, 1999, p. D1.